# crazy
## *sexy*
## juice

## ALSO BY KRIS CARR

*Crazy Sexy Love Notes* (card deck)*

*Crazy Sexy Kitchen: 150 Plant-Empowered Recipes to Ignite
a Mouthwatering Revolution* (with Chad Sarno)*

*Crazy Sexy Diet: Eat Your Veggies, Ignite Your Spark,
and Live Like You Mean It!*

*Crazy Sexy Cancer Tips*

*Crazy Sexy Cancer Survivor: More Rebellion
and Fire for Your Healing Journey*

*Available from Hay House

**PLEASE VISIT:**

Hay House USA: www.hayhouse.com®

Hay House Australia: www.hayhouse.com.au

Hay House UK: www.hayhouse.co.uk

Hay House India: www.hayhouse.co.in

# crazy
# sexy
# juice

### 100+ simple juice, smoothie & nut milk recipes to supercharge your health

## Kris Carr

FOOD PHOTOGRAPHY BY KATE LEWIS | COVER PHOTOGRAPHY BY BILL MILES

**HAY HOUSE, INC.**
Carlsbad, California • New York City
London • Sydney • Johannesburg
Vancouver • Hong Kong • New Delhi

HAY
HOUSE

Published and distributed in the United States by: Hay House, Inc.: www
.hayhouse.com® • Published and distributed in Australia by: Hay House
Australia Pty. Ltd.: www.hayhouse.com.au • Published and distributed in
the United Kingdom by: Hay House UK, Ltd.: www.hayhouse.co.uk • Pub-
lished and distributed in the Republic of South Africa by: Hay House SA
(Pty), Ltd.: info@hayhouse.co.za • Distributed in Canada by: Raincoast
Books: www.raincoast.com • Published in India by: Hay House Publishers
India: www.hayhouse.co.in

INDEXER: Laura Ogar

Food photography © Kate Lewis 2015. Prop and food styling by Kate Lewis. Food
photography assistants: Melanie Buonavolonta & Devin Echle. Cover photo, page
11, 33, and 323 © Bill Miles. All other photos © Kris Carr

Library of Congress Cataloging-in-Publication Data

Carr, Kris.
Crazy sexy juice : 100+ simple juice,
smoothie & nut milk recipes to
supercharge your health / Kris Carr.
pages cm

ISBN 978-1-4019-4152-9 (hardback)

1.  Body image. 2.  Diet. 3.  Nutrition.
4.  Reducing diets.  I. Title.

BF697.5.B63C357 2015

613.2'5--dc23

2015015287

10 9 8 7 6 5 4 3 2 1

1st edition, October 2015

Printed in the United States of America

DESIGN BY KARLA BAKER

**FOR BUDDY AND LOLA,**
my adopted fur children who give me
endless joy and remind me to add heaping
servings of wild fun to my life. And for
all of my wonderful readers, may you
love the skin you're in and be kind to
your precious selves.

Cheers to a long and vibrant life!

# CONTENTS

# welcome, gorgeous!

I am so happy you're joining me on this juicing and blending adventure. Get ready to be hooked on one of the healthiest habits around. *Crazy Sexy Juice* is your ultimate guide to the wonderful world of fruit and vegetable elixirs. The 100+ recipes in this book are over-the-moon delicious and nutritious, and range from fruity and refreshing summery potions to clean green healers, savory and spicy elixirs, creamy nut milks, and hearty superfood smoothies. If you're like me, it will be love at first sip!

No matter what stage of life we're in, we all want to feel awesome. We want to meet our full potential as we sail through our days with balance and ease. But many of us just don't know how to get there. In each of my books I've emphasized the importance of getting back to nature and the garden. Nature is the answer, dear friends. It has the power to restore and revitalize our bodies at the deepest level. A vibrant lifestyle doesn't have to be complicated, take a ton of time (and money), or add to your busy to-do list. You don't need to overhaul your kitchen or feel restricted. By simply adding these nutrient-dense beverages to your daily life, you'll be making health deposits (instead of withdrawals) and establishing a solid foundation for well-being. In fact, juicing and blending can be one of the easiest ways to achieve the freedom and vitality we seek.

Say hello to sustainable energy, glowing skin, and improved digestion. Say good-bye to inflammation, a lackluster appearance, and excess weight. Want to strengthen your immune system during cold season? Facing a health challenge and looking for a way to contribute to your well-being? Think of your green juices and smoothies as your personal pick-me-up in a glass.

We're gonna go deep because that's how I roll. I've left no stone unturned in this juicy manual for guzzling your way to glamorous (inside and out), and I can't wait for you to experience the goodness firsthand. I'll guide you through my handy tips and tricks learned over a decade of trial and triumph in the kitchen. In addition to expanding your kitchen repertoire with all the fabulous recipes in this book, you'll also get some serious brain food (AKA knowledge) so you can triumph on your own.

Here are a few of the topics we'll explore:

- The benefits and philosophy behind juicing and blending and the difference between the two. Plus, how to determine what's best for your lifestyle, schedule, and health needs

- How to create flavor combinations that tantalize your palate

- How to choose the best juicer, blender, and kitchen tools

- Ways to save money while prioritizing fresh, organic produce

- Suggestions for juicing and blending on the go

- Troubleshooting advice for common kitchen mishaps

- Tips for selection, storage, and preparation of the ingredients found in this book

- Top nutrients and health benefits of your produce, superfoods, and other ingredients

- Answers to frequently asked questions and health concerns

- Self-care hints to nurture your body and soul

- Tips on how to get your family on board and make this lifestyle stick

- And so much more . . .

If you're interested in reconnecting to your body and reinvigorating your system, I've included an easy and energizing three-day cleanse toward the end of the book. This plan is for everyone: folks who are just getting started with juices and smoothies, juicing and blending pros, and those of you who love the taste of these drinks but sometimes find it challenging to stick with the habit.

Junk and convenience foods seduce us all. Giving ourselves a healthy reboot (AKA cleanse) can bring us back to center and sanity. Think of it as an opportunity to reset your digestion and polish the already magnificent diamond that is you! This cleanse isn't about starvation, deprivation, or calorie counting: it's about recalibrating our palates and renewing our bodies by introducing cleaner, healthier foods into our lives.

During the three-day cleanse you'll enjoy a variety of delicious juices, smoothies, nut milks, and, yes, actual food that's both nourishing and satisfying—because we all love to chew. I don't know about you, but I get "hangry" (AKA hungry and angry) when my belly grumbles.

Simple steps can lead to profound change. One sip at a time, you can improve your life and your family's lives. It's happened to me and it can happen to you. When I first started sharing my journey online, I was amazed at the feedback and testimonials that came in as my story and teachings grew in popularity. Today, thousands of people have embraced the healthy habits I write about, and the results have been both heartwarming and remarkable. Reducing inflammation, healing chronic conditions, getting off excess medications, breaking free from the aches and pains that diminish our quality of life—the list grows by the day. The best part? People have been getting their joy back. What started as a tiny blog has turned into a hub of health and happiness with over a million readers every month. Sometimes I wish I could go back in time and tell my younger self that it would all be okay. Yet, at my darkest hour, I probably wouldn't have listened.

# My Crazy Sexy Story

Like some of you, I found these healthy lifestyle practices when I was in a personal crisis. Isn't that how so many transformations occur? We get knocked to our knees and decide to look for a better way. If you've been a part of my community for a while, then you probably know my story. In case you don't, here's the Cliffs Notes version: On Valentine's Day of 2003, I was diagnosed with a rare and incurable (yet thankfully slow-growing) stage IV cancer.

I was scared and didn't know where to turn. Living with an incurable disease can feel very disempowering, like there's nothing you can do to make your life better. After considerable depression, I pulled myself up by my bootstraps and took action. For years I had been feeling like garbage—I was sick, tired, and emotionally stuck. I struggled with disordered eating and low self-esteem. Basically, I didn't value myself very much, and I certainly didn't know what to eat or drink or how to deal with the toxic emotions and limiting beliefs that were holding me back.

For me, cancer put everything into focus. It helped me stop putting off a brighter day and a better tomorrow. If I couldn't be cured, could I still be healthy? Could I feel good in the skin I'm in, regardless of my medical condition? Could my heart be filled with joy and gratitude for my life and the world around me even though my plans had taken a drastic

turn? The answer was a full-blown, Technicolor HECK YES. Suddenly I felt excited. Why wait? Live now. Love now. Go for it.

That pivotal decision kicked off my own personal wellness revolution. It brought me back to nature and closer to the people and animals I love so much. If you'd asked me to drink my greens in my 20s, I would've said no thanks, and reached for a martini instead. Let's be real—my biggest connection to chlorophyll was the potted spider plant sitting in the window of my New York City apartment.

Cut to today, years after I took off for Upstate New York, armed with a juicer, a blender, and a big ole bag of greens. My juices and smoothies continue to be a big part of my daily wellness practice. This simple habit—buying or growing vegetables, washing, prepping, and creating my elixir of the day—keeps me nourished and energized. It's been my gateway to truly feeling that connection between my health, the earth, and all its beings. And that, my friends, has kept me true to caring for the world and myself each and every day. It's the backbone of my wellness practice, and I'm eternally grateful to have discovered and embraced this ritual with my whole heart.

If you've read some of my previous books, including *Crazy Sexy Cancer Tips, Crazy Sexy Diet,* and *Crazy Sexy Kitchen,* then you know that my diet is plant-based, which means it's loaded with a whole lot of greens, vegetables, fruits, nuts, seeds, legumes, and whole grains. Adjusting to a new way of eating takes motivation and a willingness to experience new tastes, textures, and flavor combinations. But if you're looking to start with a single dietary improvement, juicing and blending take the cake (so to speak).

I'm excited to share these practices with you. While this book isn't meant to be a cure-all, or a replacement for medical advice or care, it is a manifesto of juicy wisdom gathered from years of research and experience. Let the benefits of these blends speak for themselves. You'll be so glad you gave them a whirl!

It's been more than a decade since my diagnosis and I continue to live a joyful, healthy life with a chronic disease. If I can do that, just think of what *you* can do!

Are you ready to dive in? Excellent! I hope you experience juicing and blending just the way I have: as an easy and delicious journey into the transformative powers of fresh, raw fruits and vegetables. Slap on an apron and let's have some fun, hot stuff!

PART ONE

getting ready
for health

# 1

# BENEFITS AND PHILOSOPHY

## Mom said it best: "Eat your vegetables!"

It's the first commandment of healthy eating, yet chowing down on fruits and veggies seems to be the suggestion that Americans struggle with most. The latest dietary guidelines call for a minimum of 2½ to 6½ cups of fruits and vegetables per day. Yet a 2010 study showed that only about 25 percent of U.S. adults meet those daily requirements (unless you count ketchup and fries). For adolescents it's even worse. Sadly, we're doing a lousy job with our fruits and veggies, and it's taking a toll on our precious health.

Fruit and vegetable consumption is associated with reduced rates of heart disease, high blood pressure, and some cancers. It's also associated with less bodily inflammation (we'll get to that soon), less stress, better immunity, and leaner weight. With our less-than-ideal fruit and veggie noshing, it's no surprise that America is leading the way with obesity, heart disease, type II diabetes, cancer, and a huge number of other chronic diseases. We're skimping on the foods that help us stay healthy and strong, while loading up on the stuff that makes us sick. And besides the impact on individuals, this way of eating has created an unsustainable crisis for the country as a whole.

As a self-proclaimed plant pusher, I'd love nothing more than to tell you that it's a breeze to prepare fresh fruits and veggies each and every miraculous day. In my ideal world, we would all have personal nannies and endless hours to have fun and take care of ourselves. But that's just not often the case. Fruits and vegetables do require some extra time and elbow grease for washing, peeling, and chopping. They also don't keep as long as processed foods and aren't as easy to travel with—cue the packaged stuff. We don't have to think about it—just open the box or bag and we're good to go, go, go.

And let's be honest, in most cases processed food is cheaper. Or at least it seems that way while standing in the checkout line. But the truth is that the actual price of bad food is much higher once you consider the health-care costs and the environmental impact. Unfortunately, government policies make it really hard for fruits and veggies to compete. Our tax dollars go toward subsidizing only a few major mega-crops, like corn (you guessed it, corn syrup!) to keep their prices low. So until broccoli can afford a lobbyist, the 99-cent happy (crappy) meal will rule for too many people.

I believe another important reason folks don't eat enough fruits and veggies is because they haven't experienced the taste of fresh, ripe produce. Try eating a just-picked tomato from a garden and compare it to the flavorless cardboard version from the supermarket. Bleh!

It's also about the way they're cooked. Many of us haven't been exposed to the full culinary wow-factor of plants. For some, scary childhood memories of Mom's mushy, overcooked broccoli tarnish its appeal. I'm pretty certain that if we could all taste vegetables that were prepared well, we'd fall deeply-madly in love with them. Watching the response to *Crazy Sexy Kitchen* is proof positive of this! But suppose you don't have much time or don't even like cooking. Suppose you don't have many resources. Suppose you've been traumatized by a nasty dish of gray lima beans. How on earth do you develop a taste for fruits, vegetables, and greens?

The answer to these questions lies within the pages of this book. It resides in these delicious, colorful, produce-packed drinks. Creative juice and smoothie combinations can taste absolutely incredible. They're a perfect way to persuade veggie-phobes to eat more produce. Plus, they're jam-packed with good stuff. Get this: it can take over a pound of fruits and vegetables to make one juice. An average green juice at Casa Carr includes a half head of romaine, a big fistful of kale, two cucumbers, a couple of green apples, lots of lemon, and a few stalks of celery. That's a lot of produce (and nourishment), and there's no way I could sit down and nosh it all at once. Run it through a juicer, though, and you have a supremely healthy (not to mention delicious) daily habit. The same goes for blending. When you're on the go, is it always realistic to sit and eat a banana, a cucumber, avocado, kale, and coconut water? Probably not—but put them all together in a quick smoothie and you've got yourself a meal.

So, if you're making an effort to flood your diet with fresh, nutrient-dense, hydrat-

ing produce, juices and smoothies are going to be your new best friends. Now let's chat about some of the incredible health benefits they offer you.

# pH: A pHabulous Guide

You'll notice me talking about "acid" and "alkaline" throughout the book. What exactly am I referring to?

The quality of our inner ecology will determine our overall health. Life is more connected than we think. Everything from the cells in our bodies to the life in the oceans is affected by pH. The term *pH* stands for "potential hydrogen" and really just means the level of acidity or alkalinity of a given substance. To get technical, pH measures the hydrogen ions in a particular solution. Solutions that contain a lot of free hydrogen ions are considered to be acidic, while fewer ions means alkaline. In our case, that "solution" refers to our body's fluids, tissues, and organs.

As with most health-related barometers, pH is all about balance. The chemistry of your body's fluids and tissues can be measured on a pH scale of 0 to 14. Seven on the pH scale is neutral. Less than 7 is considered acidic, and greater than 7 is alkaline. Our cells are happy, healthy, and at their peak performance when living in a slightly alkaline environment. Because of that, our bodies hover in the 7.365 to 7.45 range. Even the slightest dip or rise in pH can have disastrous consequences, so our bodies are programmed to maintain that slightly alkaline threshold of 7.365 no matter what—it's basically set in stone.

Here's the potential rub: the standard American diet (SAD) is filled with acidic foods and substances, including dairy, meat, highly processed food products, and refined sugar, not to mention environmental toxins. Some research suggests that, in order to keep your pH in balance, your body will have to work harder to neutralize the acidic load, which can result in a gradual degeneration of health. Other research claims that our diets don't matter because the body will correct itself without cost to our health. So what's true? Who knows—the jury is still out. But we do know that kidney stones and gout are associated with high acid diets, so obviously there's something to pH and

food. So why not tip the scale in the alkaline direction?

The easiest way to do that is to minimize the overly acid-forming offenders (refined sugars and grains, processed foods, dairy, meat) and to maximize alkaline-forming, mineral-rich foods. These include dark leafy greens, wheatgrass, veggies, green juices, smoothies, and certain grains. Eating these goodies will flood our bodies with alkalinity and a hefty dose of vitamins and other micronutrients.

Do we have to eat alkaline foods 100 percent of the time? No way, and that's actually not possible for good health. Don't think of it as good and bad or black and white. There are definitely shades of gray. Some foods that are slightly acidic, like beans, grains, and nuts, are essential for proper nutrition on a plant-powered diet. Again, it's the *highly* acidic foods that we should limit as much as possible. Plus, life wouldn't be as fun without the occasional morning joe or slice of birthday cake. Overall, our goal is to make more energy deposits than withdrawals. Our bodies forgive the detours and exploration, as long as they don't take place 24-7.

# Taming the Flames: Inflammation

Inflammation is a hot topic that's often written about online and in magazines. While it can certainly damage our health, inflamma-

tion is actually a normal part of our body's defense system against injury or attack. The swelling and redness you get around a cut, for example? That's inflammation at work. The swelling is an attempt to isolate pesky bacteria and prevent infection. The release of histamines, which are commonly associated with allergies, is another example of an inflammatory reaction. In this case, the histamines help to dilate blood vessels, which allows our white blood cells to reach and destroy bacteria, allergens, and other microscopic particles that cramp our style.

Clearly, inflammation is necessary and vital to our well-being. But the problem arises when improper diet and lifestyle choices cause it to run amok. Instead of serving as a natural response to trauma, injury, or infection, it takes up permanent residence in our bodies, wreaking havoc on our health. Chronic pain, allergies, hay fever, atherosclerosis (AKA hardening of the arteries—often a precursor to heart disease), and even some cancers are associated with chronic inflammation. Inflammation can also show up along with other health conditions, like autoimmune diseases.

While chronic and systemic inflammation can be tricky to manage, certain positive lifestyle practices are very effective in helping tame it. Stress reduction is at the top of the list. Stress, along with long-term depression and anxiety, is associated with higher levels of inflammatory response. Meditation, positive affirmations, walks with friends, reading, laughing, sleeping or napping, painting,

journaling, singing, shaking your booty—all of these activities help tame the flames that bring us down. Exercise and adequate sleep are especially critical, as is weight management. Weight gain and excess body fat can signal a crisis to your system, throwing inflammatory responses into high gear.

Diet can be your best ally in turning off inflammation. Foods can either stoke or fight the fires of systemic inflammation. Foods that contribute to inflammation include (you guessed it!) refined sugars, processed grains, junk food, meat, and dairy—not surprisingly, the very same foods that fall on the acidic side of the pH scale. See a pattern here?

Meanwhile, the same foods that can help to keep our pH balance healthy and flood our body with nutrients are also our best allies in the fight against systemic inflammation. Fruits and vegetables—especially dark,

leafy greens—are some of the most potent anti-inflammatory agents known. The more of them you eat, the more you'll be able to switch your inflammatory response to the "off" position, resulting in a better quality of life. If you're dealing with a health condition that's linked to chronic inflammation—such as autoimmune diseases, arthritis, allergies, or heart disease—then this is the perfect time for you to be immersing yourself in the exciting world of green drinks. Other plant-based inflammation fighters include sweet potatoes, olive oil, walnuts, flax, certain spices, and organic soy.

# Powerful Prevention: Phytonutrients

Think of phytonutrients as your personal bodyguards against free radicals and diseases that threaten your health on a daily basis. Phytonutrients give plant foods (and only plant foods: you can't find them in animal products) their show-stopping colors. These natural chemicals have been associated with better eye health, immunity, and prevention of a host of different types of cancer. (Yay!)

Here are just a few notable phytonutrients:

♡ ANTHOCYANINS —compounds that create blue, purple, and red hues in foods like eggplants, blueberries, cherries, red onions, and grapes—have been associated with reduced risk of cardiovascular disease.

♡ CAROTENOIDS give veggies red, orange, and yellow hues. They're associated with eye health (if you ever wondered why you've been told to munch on carrots for better vision) and are antiaging. Find them in peppers, carrots, and winter squash.

♡ ELLAGIC ACID, found in berries and pomegranates, may help to slow the growth of cancer cells. It may even help your liver to neutralize cancer-promoting compounds.

♡ GLUCOSINOLATES, found in cruciferous veggies, may be potent cancer fighters.

♡ HESPERIDIN, found in citrus fruits, has been shown to help reduce inflammation.

♡ LUTEIN —found in green, leafy vegetables like spinach, kale, and collards—helps to prevent eye diseases, including cataracts and macular degeneration.

♡ LYCOPENE, associated with red and pink fruits and vegetables, may lower the risk of prostate cancer. You'll find it in tomatoes, watermelon, and grapefruit.

♡ PHYTOESTROGENS —found in soy foods, flax seeds, and sesame seeds— mimic the effect of estrogen very mildly in the body. They've been shown to help with menopause, and they're also associated with a reduced risk of bone loss and a reduced risk of cancer.

♡ QUERCETIN —found in apples, berries, kale, and onions—may help reduce people's risk of asthma.

♡ **RESVERATROL**, found in purple-stained fruits and vegetables (blueberries, grapes), is anti-inflammatory, and it's even been associated with life extension in certain studies.

The list goes on, but you get the bright idea: you want these incredible, potent compounds in your belly. And you guessed it again—juices and smoothies are a perfect vehicle. If you want to know more about which fruits and vegetables are particularly rich in phyto-goodness, check out the list of superstar ingredients starting on page 65.

# Hydration and Elimination

Did you know that approximately 63 million people in North America are constipated? Ouch! One study puts the prevalence at 27 percent of our population. That's a lot of backed-up and cranky folks, and we all know what that feels like: headachy, bloated, and uncomfortable.

The war on a stagnant pooper has to be waged on two fronts. First, we need more fiber. Like phytonutrients, fiber is found only in plant foods. Because we can't actually digest fiber, it passes right through us, taking all sorts of nasty debris with it, including harmful bacteria, excess cholesterol, and stagnant waste. (Pee-ew!) Consuming dietary fiber is associated with a strong immune system, a healthy balance of gut bacteria, reduced cholesterol, and a reduced

risk of heart disease. Fiber also helps control the way our bodies use sugar, which keeps appetite and blood sugar in check (and helps prevent blood sugar–related illnesses like metabolic syndrome and type II diabetes). Perhaps most important, we can't keep our elimination moving without the stuff. Low-fiber diet? A stopped-up system.

Thanks to the vegetable deficit we've already touched on, the average American gets only half of his or her recommended daily dose of fiber. (No wonder we can't go!) The solution is simple: eat (and drink) more plants; poop more.

Keep in mind that when we eat lots of healthy fiber, we also have to increase our consumption of water. Think of fiber as the stuff that helps bulk up your BMs; water is what helps keep the trains moving. One of the overlooked benefits of fruits and vegetables is that they're incredibly hydrating (unlike refined carbs and meat and processed junk, which actually dehydrate us). Getting more fruits and vegetables—especially in juice or smoothie form—can help keep our systems flooded with hydration. And drinking water throughout the course of your day is an important and easy habit. Even if you're loading up on smoothies and juices, you still need some garden-variety $H_2O$ to keep things moving!

# Sugar

How many times have you heard a friend, colleague, or neighbor complain about a sweet tooth? The fact is, more and more people are struggling with sugar addictions these days, and it's easy to see why. Americans eat *a lot* of sugar—over 150 pounds of *added* sugar per person, per year. Try hauling that around in your Halloween bag!

The American Heart Association recommends that we get no more than half of our discretionary calories (AKA extra calories our bodies don't need to function) from added sugars. This comes to about 26 to 32 grams of added sugar per person, per day, or about 6 to 8 teaspoons of added sugar. Sadly, the vast majority of Americans exceed the AHA's guideline significantly.

I've said it before and I'll say it again: you are sweet enough, darling. Consuming too much sugar (especially the processed stuff) isn't self-loving or nurturing. In fact, it can add up to some pretty serious medical life lemons. Excessive sugar consumption is associated with obesity, metabolic syndrome, heart disease, type II diabetes, and cancer. To make matters worse, it's nearly impossible to avoid in the grocery aisles. Sugar—which you may also see labeled as sucrose, maltose, corn syrup, malt syrup, dextrose, maltodextrin, high fructose corn syrup, or glucose solids—hides in nearly all processed foods, from pizza to salad dressing to spaghetti sauce to lunch meats. It's our favorite food additive, and it may be our most addictive . . . and deadly.

But here's the good news: you can take charge of your health and help protest the overabundance of sugar in our food system by becoming a more sugar-savvy consumer.

Begin by doing more of your own cooking, so you can avoid all the sugar-laden products and processed foods that fill our grocery stores. Start to cut back on added sugars (table sugar, corn syrup, malt syrup, sucrose, and artificial sweeteners) as much as possible. Finally, learn to satisfy your sweet cravings with fruits and vegetables, which are nature's own perfect sweets.

It's important to understand that all sugar is not created equal. One response to the sugar epidemic is to deem *all* sugars off-limits, but there's a big difference between natural sugars and added sugars. The reason that government agencies and health experts make a point of discouraging "added sugars" is because these types of sugars are heavily processed and devoid of any natural nutrients. They bring our blood sugar up without supplying our bodies with anything healthful: a lose-lose situation.

Naturally occurring sugars, on the other hand—I'm talking about the sugars in fresh fruits and vegetables—deliver sweetness while also providing vitamins, minerals, and concentrated stores of powerhouse phytonutrients. The sugars in fruit (or sweeter vegetables, like carrots, beets, and sweet potatoes) also come packaged with fiber, which helps us feel full and slows the absorption of sugar into our bloodstream. Plus, the micronutrients in fresh fruit may prevent the uptake of sugar in our small intestine. This means that we can enjoy the delightful sweetness and health benefits of fresh fruit without having to worry about mood-busting highs and lows and blood sugar spikes. Not surprisingly, evidence shows that populations who eat more fruit have a lower BMI and lower risk of developing many chronic diseases, including high blood pressure, heart disease, stroke, certain cancers, type II diabetes, digestive diseases, and obesity.

Of course, if you have special reason to be vigilant about the amount of sugar in your diet—for example, if you're a cancer patient or you have diabetes—then you may want to exercise some mindfulness even with naturally occurring sugars. For you, it may be wise to seek out fruits that are lower in sugar, and to use only moderate amounts of fruit and sweet veggies in your green drinks. A lot of juice and smoothie recipes out there are on the supersweet side of the spectrum, and with that in mind, I give you a range of options and plenty of resources for taking control of the sweetness of your green

elixirs. On page 49, you'll find my tips for balancing fruits and veggies in your juices and smoothies, along with some pointers on how to reduce the sugar in any recipe you love. Finally, I'll teach you all about the glycemic index and glycemic load, measurement systems that can help you to figure out which fruits are more suitable for you and your health needs.

# Fats & Protein

We need good quality fats and protein to thrive and, luckily, the plant kingdom provides them in abundance. Essential fatty acids (omega 3, 6, and 9) are necessary for your nervous system, your immune function, and your reproductive and cardiovascular systems. They also play a vital role in cell membrane function and formation, allowing nutrients and oxygen to be absorbed and waste to be excreted.

Most fruits and veggies contain trace amounts of these fatty acids. Others, like coconut, avocado, hemp, flax, and raw nuts and seeds contain an abundant amount of these life-sustaining nutrients. The days of being scared of fat are long over. We now know that fat is a crucial component to a healthy diet, and you'll find a well-proportioned amount of it in these recipes, especially the smoothies.

Protein helps build and repair tissues. It's used to make hormones and enzymes and is important for cell function. Your gorgeous hair and nails are basically made of protein.

But although we can't function without it, many people are getting more protein than they actually need, and from poor quality sources like factory-farmed meats.

Contrary to popular belief, animal products aren't the only source of protein. Nuts, nut milks, avocado, and even leafy greens are all great sources too. In fact, hemp and chia seeds are considered complete sources of protein. If you regularly include these ingredients along with beans and grains in your diet, you'll be doing a great job at meeting your body's need for protein.

Another benefit of healthy fats and proteins is that they keep you fuller and more satisfied longer. They also help slow down the absorption of sugar into your bloodstream, thus minimizing insulin spikes that tax your system.

Now that you've brushed up on some basic nutrition nuggets, let's get the skinny on juicing and blending, what appliances you'll need, how to craft a perfect elixir on your own, and other handy tips. Knowledge is power in life and in the kitchen. By the time you're done reading this book and exploring these recipes, you'll be a wealth of wisdom and a fountain of youth.

## NUT BUTTER

When buying nut butters, do your best to keep them raw. When nuts are roasted using high heat, the oils are damaged and can often go rancid. Also, avoid products with added sugars (especially the fake stuff).

# 2

# JUICING AND BLENDING, DEMYSTIFIED

What's the difference between juicing and blending? If I had a buck for every time someone asked me that question, I'd be able to stock your fridge with organic produce for life. Each method has its unique perks, but rest assured they're both fabulous ways to incorporate nutrition-packed produce into your diet.

Juicing extracts the liquid from the fruits and vegetables, leaving the fiber behind. By removing the fiber, all of the nutrients in the plant's juice—vitamins, minerals, enzymes—instantly flood our bodies with goodness. Just think of the added volume of veggies you can pack in your belly, sweet unicorns! Even those of us with the heartiest of appetites would find it challenging to consume the same amount of raw vegetables and fruits with a fork.

Juicing also gives your digestive system a little rest, and since your body works hard on your behalf 24-7, it's nice to give it some R&R. "But I thought fiber was good for you?" Yes, beautiful, you're right. And if you're upgrading your overall diet to include whole foods, you'll be getting plenty of it—especially if you include smoothies and healthy, home-cooked chow. My books *Crazy Sexy Kitchen* and *Crazy Sexy Diet* are great primers if you need more of a plan (and mouthwatering recipes).

Got digestive ouchies? Juicing is a great option for folks who love to eat plant-rich diets but whose digestive systems are too sensitive to handle lots of fiber. If that's you, juicing ensures you can enjoy the benefits of boatloads of awesome produce without suffering any tummy troubles for your efforts. For people focused on healing or repair in general, juices offer maximum health benefits in a gentle, easy-to-digest, easy-to-assimilate form.

Blending on the other hand . . . blends! The ingredients are whirled and pureed into scrumptious smoothies, fiber and all, providing the benefits of fruits and veggies along with their heart-healthy, gut-friendly fiber.

Folks who are watching their blood sugar sometimes prefer blending to juicing because the fiber ensures a slow and steady absorption of sugar into your bloodstream. It's definitely possible to create juice blends that are lower in sugar (for more information, turn to page 53), but if you feel that smoothies are a more appropriate option for you, that's fine. The important thing is to get green drinks in your diet. Take your time and experiment with both juices and smoothies to discover which one or what combination of the two is right for you and your health needs. In a typical week, my morning concoctions are usually split about 50/50 between juicing and blending. But it's not a hard and fast rule; I go with my "gut," so to speak.

Besides all the great fiber, smoothies allow you to use fantastic foods that would piss your juicer off. Take sprouts, for instance, those tiny powerhouses of plant nutrition. Sprouts will shoot right through a centrifugal juicer without getting juiced, but they blend up perfectly in smoothies. Nut butters and superfood powders can give you (and your energy levels) a powerful boost, but they can't be juiced. Blend them up, though, and you're on your way to all sorts of unusual, flavorful, and even medicinal drinks. (See page 195 for some of my favorite health-lifting smoothie formulas.)

Smoothies have another important advantage, which is that they can help you feel fuller longer. Protein, healthy fats, and carbs create sustainable energy. If you fill up your smoothies with lots of nutrient-packed ingredients, they can even serve as well-rounded, convenient, and delectable meals.

Did I mention snacks? Smoothies can work as an afternoon snack or a refreshing sip on a sizzling summer day. The fun thing about smoothies is that you can choose your own adventure: add healthy fat and protein for a meal or postworkout-worthy treat, or keep things light for a midmorning revitalizer.

Smoothies are also a great way to sneak veggies into finicky kids' meals, or to help your family (or yourself) develop a taste for leafy greens. Yet another great advantage to blending is time. Blending is faster than juicing, without a question, and the cleanup is a snap, too.

The bottom line is that both juicing and blending are wonderful and efficient ways to maximize your consumption of

the good stuff: greens, vegetables, fruits, and superfoods. One has fiber, the other doesn't. One allows for maximal nutrient intake in one sitting, while the other allows you to incorporate a wide range of ingredients and take advantage of fiber, protein, and healthy fats. Over time, you'll probably find yourself enjoying both types of drinks according to your schedule, appetite, and mood, and that's great—it's hard to go wrong when you're flooding your body with alkaline goodness! Choose what makes you happy and motivated to drink your way to wellness.

Now, let's dive a little deeper into the juicing and blending processes.

# All About Juicing

So here you are at the start of your juicing journey. You're probably wondering what juicer you'll need, how to create juices that

are as delicious as they are healthful, and how to prep and store your juice so that it's as fresh as possible. I've got you covered. But before we jump into that, let's talk schedule.

A lot of people ask me what the best time of day to juice is. My answer: Whatever time works for you, tootsie! There are no rules; it all depends on your schedule and lifestyle. But there are some ways to create a routine that fits your rhythms.

Morning is my favorite time to juice because it starts my day off with a boost of alkaline, plant-powered nourishment. It also gives me energy and helps me resist the lure of coffee—a less nourishing, more acidic way to kick off the day (though I do worship a good cup o' joe from time to time).

If mornings are too hectic for you (kids, partners, dogs, ponies), and you're able to take an afternoon break, then make that your ritual. Afternoons are an excellent time to sip some plant-powered goodness, especially if you find yourself hunting down sugary snacks when the 2 to 4 P.M. energy slump hits. A yummy juice will curb your enthusiasm for a donut, put some pep in your step, and blow away brain fog until din- nertime.

If you come home from work and find yourself immediately reaching for that bottle of Chardonnay and a bag of chips, then make a green juice and sip on it as you prep dinner. Pour it into a lavish cocktail glass, as I do. Presentation also helps lift the mood, darling.

If all else fails, consider investing in the type of juicer that allows you to prep your morning juice one night in advance (don't worry . . . I'll explain), and then sip it on the way to work.

## Choosing a Juicer

There are plenty of green machines on the market to satisfy any budget, although the cheapest ones may not always make you happiest. Think of your juicer purchase as an investment in your long-term wellness, energy, and radiance. We want to squeeze every possible ounce of goodness into our glasses. Unfortunately, crappy juicers can produce crappy yield. If you're going to spend money on high-quality, organic fruits and vegetables, and time preparing them for juicing, you might as well be sure that the machine you use helps maximize their nutrients and power.

In general, there are two main categories of juicers for noncommercial use. I'll explain them more thoroughly in a moment, but the basic difference is that one works quickly and is easy to clean but isn't necessarily top- of-the-line when it comes to the longevity of your juices. The other creates juices that may contain more nutrients and enzymes and can keep for a few days, but takes more time and can be harder to clean than its quicker counterparts.

Frankly, the choice you make depends on your goals and your lifestyle. If you're a hard- core raw foodie who wants to invest in a killer machine and you have some extra time on your hands, you might go full tilt with a masticating or twin gear juicer. On the other hand, if you're a working *mamacita* who knows that she's going to make her green juice only if it's relatively quick and easy to clean up, then you might opt for a centrifugal model. Will there be some compromise in nutritional value if you go the easier way? Sure. But it all comes down to whether or not you'll actually commit to juicing. So for best results, choose the juicer you'll actually use!

Since everyone has different needs and budgets, I want to show you how I evaluate the many juicers on the market today so that you can choose a juicer that fits your life. That said, make sure to read reviews and do your own research.

## Centrifugal Juicers

My centrifugal juicer is my go-to companion. I love it mostly because it's fast and easy (like some of my old boyfriends). Centrifugal juicers have a wide mouth to feed your fruits and veggies into, which means you don't have to cut produce into itty-bitty pieces beforehand. Big timesaver.

### OXIDATION

What really separates these machines is how much opportunity they create for a process called *oxidation* to occur. Oxidation is what happens when a substance—anything from metal to living tissue to produce—is exposed to (you guessed it!) oxygen. The oxygen causes the substance in question to lose electrons. This can be good or bad, but in the case of fresh fruits and veggies, oxidation typically results in spotting, browning, or other symptoms of aging.

Not surprisingly, juicers that expose vegetables to a lot of air during the juicing process, like centrifugal juicers, allow more oxidation to take place than machines that limit the amount of oxygen exposure to your fruits and veggies. The result is juices that have a shorter shelf life. To maximize the flavor and freshness of these green drinks, be sure to drink 'em as soon as you can.

So, how do these babies work? Your veggies and fruits are pushed through a chute into a fast-spinning mesh basket with a grated bottom. The produce is shredded and spun, sending the juice through the mesh and into a pitcher while the pulp goes into a separate basket. Voilà!

On the downside, they're pretty loud, and the high-speed spinning causes the juice to oxidize faster than it would with slower speed juicers. For this reason, it's best to drink juices from a centrifugal juicer right away to ensure the most nutrients and best flavor and color. However, if saving some juice for later means that you drink more juice, then by all means store your juice in an airtight mason jar and keep it in the fridge till you're ready to enjoy it—I won't tell the health police. But know that centrifugal juices probably won't last overnight—at least not with their fresh flavor intact. They also aren't very good with certain leafy greens, sprouts, or herbs. But as you'll soon learn, there are some helpful tips for maximizing the yield on these delicate ingredients.

Popular choices for centrifugal juicers: Breville Ikon Multi-Speed, Breville Juice Fountain Compact (a smaller juicer, great for apartment living), and the Omega 4000. While I haven't tried all the choices on the market today, many of my readers also love the Cuisinart Juice Extractor, the Hamilton Beach Big Mouth Pro, and the newer versions of the popular and affordable Jack LaLanne machines. Once again, do your research before you invest and make sure there's a good return policy if you're unsatisfied.

## Masticating Juicers (AKA Slow Juicers)

These lovelies operate a bit like our pearly whites—they use a single gear (or auger) that chews up your produce in order to break down the fibrous cell walls and extract the juice, which is gently squeezed through a stainless steel screen. Masticating juicers tend to have a higher yield than centrifugal juicers, and therefore dryer pulp. Because they run at slower speeds, you'll get less oxidation and more nutrients. Plus the juice lasts longer. Store it in a tightly sealed

mason jar and refrigerate, and it should keep for up to 48 hours. Score! And if noise is a concern, masticating juicers are the way to go. They purr like kittens.

Popular choices for masticating juicers: Hurom Slow Juicer (my personal favorite, which includes a 10-year warranty), Omega 8006 Nutrition System Juicer, Omega VRT350, Breville Fountain Crush Slow Juicer, Champion Household Juicer.

## Twin Gear Juicers (AKA Triturating Juicers)

Twin gear juicers operate at even slower speeds than masticating juicers, which means these rock star machines extract the highest yield and retain the most nutrients in your liquid sunshine. They grind and press the produce between two interlocking roller gears and slowly squeeze out the goodness. Because there's less oxidation, you'll get up to 72 hours of nutrient-rich juice—provided you store your juice in an airtight container and keep it in the fridge. The other advantage of twin gear juicers (and masticating juicers) is that they make the most of leafy greens and even wheatgrass, which, as I mentioned earlier, don't yield as much juice when processed with centrifugal machines. You can even make nut butters in these bad boys.

Both masticating and twin gear juicers are powerful, health-producing machines but they have a few downsides: the whole

## WHEATGRASS

Wheatgrass gets an Olympic gold medal in health. Widely acclaimed for its nutritional and therapeutic properties, wheatgrass is teeming with phytonutrients—specifically antioxidants, which help keep aging and degeneration at bay. Wheatgrass may help protect the liver against alcohol damage and oxidative stress, and it may also help regulate blood sugar. Basically, wheatgrass has got it going on, and you'd be wise to get your hands on it.

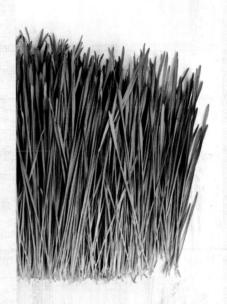

Wheatgrass is surprisingly easy to come by: many health stores carry it, and you can even get a shot at Jamba Juice and Whole Foods coffee and smoothie bars. There are home delivery services, and it's also easy (and cheap) to grow.

Centrifugal juicers can't handle wheatgrass, so don't bother. You'll create mess and mayhem. In order to juice wheatgrass, you'll need a masticating or twin gear juicer or a hand-crank model.

Wheatgrass juicers work by slowly squeezing juice out of the tough wheatgrass fibers—similar to wringing out your wet clothes after running through the sprinkler.

Popular choices for hand-crank juicers: Lexen Healthy Juicer, Z-Star Manual Juicer, Chef's Star Manual Hand Crank, Handy Pantry HJ Hurricane. For electric versions, see my recommendations for masticating and twin gear juicers.

Wheatgrass may not taste like sunshine, but it will make you glow from the inside out. By the way, taking a sip of orange, pineapple, or apple juice as a chaser will help to balance out wheatgrass's eau de earthiness.

process of making a juice tends to take a bit longer than centrifugal. The prep involves cutting the produce into smaller sizes because their mouths are typically narrow. Feeding the juicer takes time because the gears turn slowly. And finally, the cleanup can include a few extra steps because there are often more parts to rinse and scrub. In addition, sometimes pulp can slip through. No biggie. You can either strain it or just enjoy the extra fiber.

These juicers are also more expensive. All that said, they're still the go-to choice for health gurus and advocates.

Consider all of these factors when you're thinking about the juicer you want; there's no point having a fancy machine if the time you need to spend cleaning it outweighs your juice craving in the first place!

Popular choices for twin gear juicers: Super Angel 5500, Samson Green Power, Green Star Elite Juice Extractor.

## ENZYMES

Enzymes are your body's workforce. They're the busy builders and demolition teams that constantly tear down and reconstruct the body. Millions of enzymes are working in your body right now to support everything from digesting your green juice to healing your paper cut.

Digestive enzymes help break down food, while metabolic enzymes run the rest of the show by orchestrating the biochemical reactions that fuel every cell in your body. High temperatures destroy enzymes, so some experts believe that maximizing your intake of raw foods and fresh juices can help to replenish your body's reserve. Plus, the enzymes in certain fruits—pineapple, for instance—have a beneficial impact on digestion.

As you select a juicer, keep in mind that masticating and twin gear models will keep more enzymes intact—and allow them to last longer—than centrifugal machines.

# Norwalk Hydraulic Press

Last but not least: the slowest, most effective badass on the scene. If you've won the lottery, robbed a bank, or inherited the family jewels from your aunt Trudy, check out the Norwalk juicer—which costs around $2500. This machine literally presses (as in uses a hydraulic press) the juice out of fruits and veggies, including tough-to-juice grasses like wheatgrass. This powerful juicer provides 50 to 100 percent more juice than other machines, and the juice itself will stay very fresh for up to three days.

Because Norwalk machines are so expensive, they're used mostly at healing centers or for commercial purposes—including the cold-pressed juices you may have come across in juice bars. You can't walk into the local Target and buy one. Generally, you have to procure them online or from a juice bar that sells them. But, hey, a gal can dream!

# Before You Select a Juicer . . .

. . . ask yourself the following questions:

What's my budget?

How much prep time am I willing to invest in my daily juicing?

How much cleanup will I be willing to do on a daily basis?

What's more important: the shelf life of my juice or the time/effort it takes to prepare it?

How much space do I have?

Will I be juicing wheatgrass?

You can't go wrong with any of the juicers I've recommended. Keep that bad boy visible so you don't forget it exists. Clean it as soon as you're done using it so it's always ready to whip up a juice. If for whatever reason you can't clean it right away, soak the parts in warm water till you're ready. This will keep them from getting crusty (and stinky) and doubling the time it takes to clean.

Plus, if you have a pushy partner or husband like I do, cleaning the juicer right away will ensure a heavenly, lecture-free morning. For centrifugal juicers that have a catch basket, you can line it with a biodegradable bag for no-fuss-or-muss cleaning. Many juicers come with a scrub brush; this is essential for cleaning the basket or the nooks and crannies of the gears. If your juicer doesn't come with a brush, grab one the next time you're at the grocery store. It's the only way you'll get that sucker clean.

Look at your juicer purchase as a fresh start. You've taken your first step toward a glowing new you! Celebrate by drinking your first green juice in a champagne glass and toast to your health.

# Crafting the Perfect Juice Combo

This book will give you plenty of inspiration for kick-ass, creative concoctions. But if you're a curious kitchen-lover like me, you'll want to build your own works of art. Here's some general guidance to help you choose the ingredients that tend to work best for crafting the perfect elixir. And don't fret— you can't make a mistake, and we'll talk all about specific ingredients in Chapter 4.

PICK YOUR BASE. The best bases are watery vegetables, which produce a lot of volume. My faves? Super-alkaline cucumber, electrolyte-rich celery, and even powerhouse broccoli stems work really well. Beets and carrots are also good, but a little goes a long way, as these root veggies contain more sugar. Of course, you don't have to pick just one base ingredient; a mixture of any of these veggies will work. The more, the merrier. Occasionally, I'll use fruit as a base for a light and fun alternative, but for the most part, watery veggies are my go-to for everyday juicing.

**PICK YOUR LOVELY LEAFIES.** Next, focus on your greens. If you're a juicing newbie, start with a few leafy greens at first, let your taste buds adjust for a few days, and then start to add more. If your juice tastes like lawn clippings, pull back. Any combination of leafy greens (kale, romaine, spinach, collards, cabbage, dandelion greens, or Swiss chard) will work. Romaine and spinach have a milder taste, so they're great for beginners or those who don't like some of the stronger greens. Daikon radish and bok choy are also great greens to experiment with.

**PICK YOUR FRUITS.** Apples, pears, pineapple, cantaloupe, citrus, and watermelon will give you the juiciest bang for your buck, but other fruits—including grapes, kiwis, cantaloupe, honeydew, and strawberries—create delicious sweetness and unusual flavors.

**PICK A KICK.** Before you finish making your juice, try adding some extra flavor in the form of herbs, spices, and tartness. Think of this like seasoning: before you bring a dish to the table, you season to taste, right? Well, now's your chance to do the same with your juice. Herbs (especially cilantro, parsley, and mint) can be the difference between juice as usual and juice that rocks your world. If you're daring, add a dash of cayenne pepper or cinnamon, so long as the flavors work. For tartness, start with tried-and-true juice tune-ups like lemon, lime, and ginger. Keep experimenting and jazzing up your juice as you go along!

## Loading Your Juicer

Once you've chosen your ingredients, it's time to juice. The order in which you load your fruits and veggies isn't crucial but it can sometimes make a difference. Ingredients that are harder to juice, or that don't produce much yield (including dark, leafy greens, ginger, herbs) should be followed by a watery vegetable or fruit, which can help these fibrous greens pass through your juicer easily. I often send my greens through first, and then add cucumber, apple, celery, or pineapple (or anything else that's super juicy) right after them.

Here's another good tip for juicing greens and herbs: roll them up or bunch them into a ball before juicing. You'll get lots more green goodness!

# All About Blending

Just like with juices, there is no best time to drink a smoothie. A tall glass of blended green goodness is my idea of a Happy Meal anytime. If only there were green smoothie drive-thrus. When I'm looking for a hearty breakfast, an easy snack during the day, or even when I'm super pressed for time and can't make a decent meal, I go the blended route. Smoothies even help quell the ole midnight Oreo Double Stuf cravings. Yes, I get them, too. Basically, there's really no right or wrong time to blend. Yay!

# Choosing a Blender

Blenders have come a long way from their piña colada beginnings. One great thing about all blenders is that they are easy to clean and there aren't as many parts or components to maintain. In general, blenders range from expensive high-speed machines to moderately priced units that will more than likely get the job done. But the best ones are worth the added cost. Trust me. Save your pennies and make it a priority to get one when you can. A top-shelf blender lasts a lifetime.

These days I'm cruisin' with the Rolls Royce of blenders—the mighty Vitamix. This big dog can blend up just about anything, including raw soups, sauces, ice cream, nut butters, and the occasional margarita. Heck, it could grind a cowboy boot, though I don't recommend it.

The Vitamix is super-easy to use. It has one switch and one dial that both allow for variable speeds. Plus, it comes with a handy plastic tamper that helps loosen ingredients that get stuck in corners. The sole drawback is the cost. These machines range from around $350 to over $600, depending on the model. Rest assured that you are investing in a quality appliance that will stick with you through years of blending adventures. If you run into some snags along the way, Vitamix provides a seven-year warranty on new models and a five-year warranty on reconditioned ones. (Yup, you can score a gently used machine.)

The Blendtec is another quality Bad Mama Jama. Blendtec prices are comparable to those of the Vitamix and they, too, offer reconditioned models, so it really boils down to personal preference. In our house, my hubby is the Blendtec guy, while I'm the Vitamix gal. Blendtec is slightly shorter and lighter than the Vitamix (easier to store in cabinets) and it comes with preprogrammed settings that basically do the thinking for you. But because it's lighter, it can skitter across the counter a bit. Some folks suggest that smoothies made with a Blendtec are frothier than the creamy versions created by a Vitamix. I haven't really noticed this, but you might. Blendtec seems to handle a full pitcher of thick liquids better than the Vitamix. One Blendtec bummer is that it doesn't handle dates very well; the little suckers end up in chunks at the bottom of the pitcher. Get in my belly, you darling date!

Another high-speed blender to choose from, that's certainly more affordable, is the Oster Versa. I sampled one recently and was really impressed with its performance. Though it was lighter weight and didn't seem as rugged, it still worked like a champ. At just under $300, it's a bargain for a high-speed machine.

If these premium blenders are out of your price range, you can still make tasty smoothies with one of the many moderately priced machines out there. These babies aren't as powerful, but as I mentioned earlier, they can get the job done—especially if you're mainly using them for smoothies. Breville,

Cuisinart, Omega, Waring, and KitchenAid all make solid machines with prices ranging from $100 to $400.

Last but not least, there are the personal blenders, of which the Magic Bullet and Nutribullet are currently the most popular. Personal blenders are small (typically for making 1 to 2 servings at a time), affordable, and easy to use. These units are great for people who are challenged for counter space or who want to make smoothies on the road. They're a snap to clean and usually come with multiple pitcher sizes and blades. The Bullets have diehard fans, and if you enjoy binge-watching infomercials as much as I do, you've probably seen these superstars on the tube. Check them out!

Another option is the Vitamix S30. This little cutie is a dynamo of power. It comes with two small containers and a mini tamper (to make life easier and smoothies blend faster). I love using it to whip up smaller smoothie batches or to make sauces and dressings. It's easier than hauling out the big boys. Don't expect to pack it in your suitcase, though. It may be small, but it's still pretty heavy.

Before buying any blender, do your homework—research, read consumer reviews, and comparison-shop for the best deal. With a little effort, you'll find a righteous beast that serves you well.

# Before You Select a Blender . . .

. . . ask yourself the following questions:

What's my budget?

How powerful does my blender need to be?

How much space do I have?

How many people am I blending for?

If you're into baubles and bonuses, many of these blenders come with accessories. Me, I'm simple. I look for a workhorse motor, good blades, and a warranty. As you rely on your blender for a variety of culinary creations, don't be surprised if stuff breaks or wears out over time. For your basic needs, a lower price-point blender can certainly do the trick. But as I mentioned before, when finances allow, you'll definitely want to upgrade. Another benefit of high-speed blenders is that they're better at pulverizing produce and extracting more nutrients from the fiber/pulp. They're also good at blending trickier ingredients like nuts and the afore-mentioned dates. FYI—soaking your nuts (I always laugh when I type that) and dates definitely makes them easier to blend.

If you have a blender with multiple speeds, give it some foreplay by starting on low and working your way up. You both will have a better experience. Above all, make sure the lid is secure. Jackson Pollock smoothie art on your walls and windows ain't cute. Another great tip is to invest in some good spatulas in various widths. These

## NUT AND SEED MILKS

As you become a blending pro, you may want to start making your own nut and seed milks. This is surprisingly easy to do, and once you get used to the rich taste of homemade blends, it'll be hard to return to the commercial stuff. (Trust me!) Making your own nut milk also means that you get to control the sweetness, while also adding all sorts of fun flavors like cocoa, cinnamon, and even turmeric. You can learn all about how to do this in Chapter 9.

You don't have to make these from scratch, though. There are a lot of great options for store-bought nut and seed milks these days, and they're multiplying by the day. Making nut milk at home gives you more control over taste and ingredients, but the most important thing is that you find a way to create these wonderful blends in the first place. If using store-bought nondairy milk helps you do that, then go for it! Be sure to purchase the "unsweetened" or "original" variety of these brands; chocolate and vanilla usually contain a lot of added sweeteners. Here are some of the brands I like most:

ALMOND MILK: Whole Foods' 365, Silk Pure Almond, Pacific Natural Foods, Califia Farms

CASHEW MILK: Cashew Dream, So Delicious Dairy Free

HAZELNUT MILK: Pacific Natural Foods

HEMP MILK: Tempt, Pacific Natural Foods

QUINOA MILK (perfect for nut and seed allergies): Suzie's

RICE MILK (another great option for those with nut and seed allergies): Rice Dream, Pacific Natural Foods

SUNFLOWER SEED MILK: Sunrich Natural's "Sol" brand, Sunflower Dream

recipes are so scrumptious you'll want to scrape out every last drop.

# Creating a Stupendous Smoothie

Like with juices, there are endless varieties and taste sensations for smoothies. Over time, you'll develop combinations that float your boat, but as you get started, it can be helpful to keep this basic advice in mind when you're choosing ingredients. These categories are mere suggestions to get your own creative juices flowing. You don't have to use them all.

PICK YOUR LIQUID BASE. Every smoothie needs a liquid base to make it easy to blend and sip. My personal preference is to use nut milks, but coconut water is great, too. If you add healthy, creamy fats to your smoothie in the form of nuts or avocado, then feel free to just use water as your base. Whatever tastes good to you.

PICK YOUR FRUITS AND VEGGIES. Which flavors would you like to shine through the most in your blend? Bananas and mangoes make particularly wonderful smoothie bases because they're creamy, sweet, and versatile (AKA they play nicely with most other fruits). Melon also makes a nice smoothie base (I'm partial to watermelon and honeydew), as do berries. Cucumber adds mild, hydrating flavor to smoothies, and avocado creates smooth, creamy texture.

Enhance your smoothie with some alkaline-powered, nutrient-rich, leafy greens. Pretty much any leafy green can be added to your blend, from spinach to chard to dandelion greens. The mildest choices are baby spinach and romaine; kale and collards have slight bitterness, but they work well, too. Chard is fairly neutral, and it'll add the slightest hint of saltiness to your smoothie. Does every smoothie have to be green? Nope—it's okay to create some blends that are more fruity-focused than green. But for a standard, everyday breakfast smoothie, green is a good way to go.

MIX AND MATCH. Don't limit your blending repertoire to a few go-to ingredients. It's boring and it's also not as healthy. Rotation and variety are key. Additional fruits and veggies can create unusual and complex flavor profiles. Banana smoothie? Tasty. Banana blueberry? Tastier. Banana mango cucumber avocado? Taste orgasm! You get the idea. Don't be afraid

to think outside the box, to experiment with wacky combinations, and to let your personality shine through. It's rare that a smoothie is so yucky that it can't be fixed, but if it's a total disaster (it happens), you can always feed it to your garden so it won't go to waste!

PICK YOUR FAT AND/OR PROTEIN. Smoothies are much more creamy and satisfying when they're infused with some sort of healthy fat or protein. I love adding avocado or even coconut butter to my green smoothies. Nuts or a tablespoon or two of nut butter are also great options that will keep you full and fueled.

If you use particularly creamy nut milk in your smoothie (like my cashew chai milk), then you may not need to add extra fat; it's up to you.

PICK YOUR BOOSTS. This is the place to get creative with superfood ingredients (like cacao, maca, or spirulina; see page 85 for more on these potent health heroes), spices (cinnamon, turmeric, ginger), and herbs (basil, cilantro, parsley). Think of these add-ins as the little touches that give your smoothie personality, pizzazz, and power.

# Packing Your Blender

For the smoothest blends, add your liquid first. Next, add your fruit and greens. Finally, add your boosts and bonuses. Anything frozen should go last because the blender blades heat up slightly and can turn the icy stuff a bit watery.

## FREEZING FRUIT

I love using frozen fruit in my smoothies. It creates thicker blends—the kind you can eat with a spoon—and makes your smoothies super cool and refreshing. Here are some of my favorite frozen fruits to use as smoothie bases:

BANANAS: I always have a bag of frozen 'naners sitting in my freezer; I peel, chop, and freeze them as soon as they're turning brown. Once again, don't forget to peel your bananas *before* freezing; the skins are almost impossible to get off once they're frozen!

MELON: Cantaloupe, honeydew, and watermelon all freeze well and add frosty texture to smoothies. I cut them into chunks, bag 'em up, and toss in the freezer.

MANGO: Bananas may be the most popular smoothie base, but for those of you who don't like bananas or are allergic to them, frozen mangoes create a similarly creamy, sweet base for smoothies.

Freezing fruit for smoothies is actually a great way to preserve ripe fruits that are perched on the cusp of going bye-bye. If I see a carton of berries that's getting slightly mushy or a banana that's turning brown, off to the freezer it goes. You'll also find bags of fruit in the freezer section of your health-food store, but pound for pound, you'll be paying more for the convenience.

Super frosty smoothies mighty feel too chilly in the dead of winter, so I often use room temperature fruit in the colder months. If you do this, you'll probably need to add less liquid than you would with frozen fruit.

# Balancing Your Fruits and Veggies

Before you use all of this beautiful new knowledge to create some stunning concoctions, I want to address the issue of balance. Many people get overwhelmed when trying to figure out how many fruits and veggies to use in their drinks. Some folks don't want too much sugar; others lean toward sweeter recipes because they don't want to be hit in the kisser by an all-kale punch. If you're hoping to keep your juices a little more balanced—and maximize your alkaline intake—then the following suggestions are for you. They'll help you to craft elixirs that feature healthy amounts of fruits and veggies.

The basic goal is to include more veggies and leafy greens than fruit in your daily routine. For instance, when I make my green lemonade (page 127), I use celery, cucumber, and leafy greens, along with one small-to-medium-sized apple—a perfect ratio of alkalizing green goodness to natural, fruity sweetness. You can extend this rule of thumb to nearly all of your green juices, and you'll quickly see that a smaller portion of fruit (or sweet, starchy veggies) goes a long way in making those powerful greens powerfully palatable.

Do you always have to use this formula? Nope, this isn't an exact science. That's why you'll find recipes in this book that don't always hold tightly to that rule. The point is to add more veggies than fruit to your juice on a regular basis. Sometimes I crave a fruity drink (like my Green & Gold, page 165, or my Pretty in Pink juice, page 167). These sweeter blends are a great way to celebrate the natural sweetness and beauty of fresh fruit. But if you want to maximize the healing powers of your juices, then it's best to keep that ratio in mind most of the time.

It can be harder to stick to this ratio of more veggies to fruit when making smoothies, but try to work vegetables into your blended beverages whenever possible. Add a heaping amount of spinach, kale, or other

## GREEN POWDERS

You may have seen commercial green powders on the market. These are usually a blend of chlorophyll, wheatgrass powder, barley grass powder, and other good green stuff. It may be tempting to use these powders in place of your own green drinks, but I recommend sticking to real produce. It's fresher and better for you than anything you can buy in a pouch.

That said, green powders are useful when you're on the go, traveling, or stuck at the office all night. Mix them into water for a boost. Green powders are also handy if you're low on veggies. My favorite brands include Amazing Grass, Aloha, and Garden of Life Perfect Food Green.

## NUT/SEED MILK ICE CUBES

Yes, you read that correctly—this next tip is wicked good. When I was a smoothie newbie, I often struggled with runny, watered-down blends. I loved adding ice to them for a cool, frosty texture, but as the ice melted, so did the flavor. (Boo!) The discovery of nut milk ice cubes transformed my world, and it can revolutionize your smoothie-making process, too.

Simply set aside an ice-cube tray or two for nut milk cubes and fill them with nut, seed, or coconut milk. Put them in the freezer, and ta-da! They'll freeze, just like regular ice cubes, resulting in the perfect blending secret weapon.

Nut milk or coconut milk ice cubes will melt as you blend them, but instead of adding water to your blend, they'll add creamy, cool, nut milk texture. Pretty magical, right?

leafy greens to your blender, or try adding cucumber. (It's magical when whipped up with banana, mango, and other tropical fruits.) Carrots or carrot juice, beets, herbs, and even broccoli make wonderful smoothie additions—I promise!

Bottom line: If focusing on fruit in your smoothies helps you to get the green stuff in, then don't worry too much about your vegetable-to-fruit ratio. But over time, see if you can get into the habit of adding more

greens. Your taste buds will adapt, and it won't be long before you're hankering to get your greens.

## The Glycemic Index & Glycemic Load

As you shift your focus away from processed sweets and toward naturally sweet fruits, it's helpful to keep a little system called the glycemic index (GI) in mind. The glycemic index is a measure of how quickly and how high a particular carbohydrate raises your blood sugar level. It's based on a numerical ranking system that compares a particular food to pure glucose (which is given a rating of 100). The closer a food's glycemic index is to 100, the more likely it is that its carbohydrates will raise blood sugar levels.

Foods with a very high GI value are almost always refined carbs—grain products, like white flour, that have had most of the fiber and nutrition stripped away, or white sugars and syrups. Conversely, foods that are low on the GI scale tend to be complex carbohydrates (think whole grains, like oats, brown rice, quinoa, and millet, or starchy root vegetables). These foods contain carbohydrates, but they don't cause blood sugar spikes the way refined carbs do, because their naturally occurring fiber and protein help to slow the entrance of sugar into the blood. Blood sugar spikes lead to insulin spikes, because insulin is the hormone that signals our body to store any sugar we don't immediately need. Over time, repeated insulin spikes can lead to weight gain and metabolic syndrome and other diseases.

When it comes to fruits, here's what you should know: lower-GI fruits include lemons, Granny Smith apples, berries, pears, grapefruit, oranges, grapes, and kiwi. Some higher-GI fruits include watermelon, grapes, bananas, pineapple, and dates.

In recent years, our understanding of the glycemic index has been refined, and another measure called the glycemic load (GL) has entered the picture. While the glycemic index only measures how quickly a carbohydrate is digested and converted into glucose in the bloodstream, the glycemic load takes into account how much of the carbohydrate we actually consume in one sitting. As it turns out, many of the fruits that have a high GI ranking actually have a low GL ranking, in part because we don't consume many of their carbohydrates per serving. Watermelon, for instance, has a GI of 72, but a GL of only 4. This is because watermelon is mostly water, so one serving actually doesn't supply us with much of the carbohydrate in question. The same goes for carrots, which have a GI of 71 but a GL of only 6. It's also true for bananas, grapes, and a number of other fruits.

So it's important to understand that a high GI ranking isn't the entire story and doesn't automatically mean that a fruit or vegetable is "bad." The glycemic load is often a better real-world indicator of how foods affect us, and it will help you compare some of your favorite juice and smoothie ingredients for their impact on blood sugar.

You can check out GI and GL rankings for a number of common foods at www.health.harvard.edu/healthy-eating/glycemic_index_and_glycemic_load_for_100_foods. For even more comprehensive information on glycemic index and glycemic load, check out *The New Glucose Revolution* by Jennie C. Brand-Miller, Ph.D.; Thomas Wolever, M.D.; Kaye Foster-Powell; and Stephen Colagiuri, M.D. Those folks are thorough! You can also

## HOW TO ADJUST THE SUGAR CONTENT OF A RECIPE

Suppose you're being especially mindful of your sugar intake, but you fall in love with a juice or a smoothie recipe that seems to be on the sweeter side. Don't worry: most recipes can be modified to decrease sugar while retaining their character and flavor.

Start by examining what the sources of sweetness in the recipe are (sweet fruits, root vegetables, etc.) and decreasing the quantity of these ingredients. For example, if a juice calls for two or three apples, try using one instead. Or use Granny Smith apples rather than a sweeter variety. The important thing is to replace the sweet ingredient with another, lower-sugar one so that your yield stays consistent. I love to use cucumber and celery to create volume and flavor in recipes with minimal sugar (and maximal nutrition!). One medium cucumber will yield about the same amount of juice as two apples or three large carrots.

In smoothies, you'll often see a lot of banana, pineapple, or mango. If you prefer, replace some or all of these fruits with lower sugar options, like kiwi, peaches, pears, grapes, or berries.

Some of the smoothie recipes in this book call for pitted dates as a sweetener. Dates are one of the most concentrated sources of sweetness that nature has to offer. (They're called "nature's candy" for a reason.) I love using them in place of conventional syrups or refined sugars because they deliver caramel-like sweetness along with fiber, potassium, and magnesium. Usually, when I include dates in recipes, I'll give you a range in suggested quantity, so you can adjust the amount to fit your taste. You can also eliminate dates altogether. You know your body best.

These same principles work in reverse. If a juice or smoothie seems to lack the sweetness you crave, feel free to add a little more fruit, sweeter root veggies, or another date (in the case of smoothies). It's best to add these ingredients slowly because once your beverage has been sweetened, it's harder to tone it down if you've gone too far.

Finally, remember that it's possible to create tons of flavor and character in recipes without relying exclusively on sweet ingredients. One of my favorite tricks for brightening the taste of my juices and smoothies is to use fresh herbs, lemon, lime, and ginger. Just because your juice or smoothie isn't sweet, doesn't mean it should be blah.

find plenty of charts and information online.

Nutrition is complicated business, and how we respond to different ingredients depends heavily on our individual constitutions as well as our overall diet and lifestyle habits. Use the GI/GL for guidance, but don't go too crazy with it. Just make an overall effort to remember which foods are a bit higher on the spectrum, and if you're working with a health challenge, use the system as a means of creating the boundaries you need.

3

# PREPPING
# YOUR
# KITCHEN

After juicing and blending for over a decade, I've found clever ways to make the process as clean, easy, and speedy as possible. The first thing you'll want to do is organize your kitchen. Create some space for your escapades and make sure your tools of the trade are accessible. Over time you'll build a system and get in a rhythm. Above all, have fun. They're just juices and smoothies!

There are a few groovy gadgets that help streamline and expedite your process. Here's a list of my most coveted little kitchen helpers:

**Canning funnel:** I have to give my hubby credit for this ingenious idea. He's a frugal fella. After your produce goes through the juicer once, send it through for a second trip. Sound messy? Pop a funnel into the juicer mouth and dump the pulp in. Finally, flush it through with a splash of water. Ta-da! You'll get at least 2 to 4 more ounces, which equals extra goodness for your body and pocketbook. They're only a few bucks and you can find them at most housewares stores.

**Cutting board:** If you already have this kitchen item—marvelous. If not, or if you're in the mood for an upgrade, try bamboo, which is easy to clean and ecofriendly. Avoid plastic cutting boards if you can: tiny pieces of the plastic can break off and find their way into your glass. Yuck!

**Debbie Meyer GreenBags:** Keep your produce fresh longer with these magical reusable bags. Less waste. Less time shopping. 'Nuff said!

**Mason jars:** These are perfect for storing smoothies and juices. Fill them to the brim and fasten the top tightly. You want as little oxygen inside as possible, since oxygen chomps away at your drink's freshness. (See my note about oxidation, page 36.) You'll find them at grocery stores, craft or hardware stores, big box stores (especially during canning season in early fall), any kitchen supply store, and even the dollar store.

**Mixing bowls:** Ooh, I love me some stainless steel mixing bowls. I collect various sizes and have them on hand for all my cooking needs. They're awesome for corralling all your ingredients and can also be used as scrap bowls for all the butts, peels, and pits that accumulate along the way.

**Nut milk bag:** A great investment if you've fallen in love with the rich taste of homemade nut milks. They're cheap, easy, and reusable. You can find them online or at most kitchen supply stores. Cheesecloth also works perfectly well for the straining process, as do very inexpensive paint strainer bags from the hardware store—just rinse before using.

popular among my chef friends, but you don't have to get super fancy. Just make sure your knives fit comfortably in your hand and you keep them sharp.

**Strainer and salad spinner:** Need I say more? These two are essential for all things Crazy Sexy.

# Grocery Shopping

Now we get to one of my favorite things—shopping! When you hit the produce aisles, natural/health-food stores, farmers' markets, and CSAs, choose a wide variety of veggies and fruits that are fresh and (in the case of fruit) ripe. Ripe fruits are in their most nutritious state. Unfortunately, most fruits and veggies are plucked before they're ready, so do your best to choose foods that are local, seasonal, and at their height of freshness. Avoid limp or slimy greens, mushy avocados (the meat should be green, not bruised), soggy berries, and spotted or overbruised apples and pears. There's a ton of information about how to pick the best produce in the next chapter, so you will be fully prepared.

If possible, try to make it to the store twice a week for produce; this isn't always easy, but it's the most surefire way to stock a fridge with fabulously fresh fruits and veggies. If you can't swing two hauls, though, don't worry: using those Debbie Meyer GreenBags I talked about can help extend the life of all of your veggies, especially delicate greens.

**Peeler:** If your fruits or vegetables aren't organic and have a skin, peel 'em, especially if they're on the Dirty Dozen list (page 60). You'll lessen the amount of pesticides that make it into your glass and your body.

**Scrub brush:** A must-have for cleaning your produce and your juicer. Veg and fruit shreds are stubborn little sons of buggers when left to dry in your machine. As I mentioned earlier, I recommend scrubbing your juicer and blender parts as soon as you finish using them. This simple act will cut your cleaning time in half!

**Sharp knife:** Want to make your life easier? Invest in a good knife. Some of your ingredients will need to be cut into smaller pieces to fit in your juicer or blender, and a high-quality knife makes the process a breeze. My favorite knives are NHS brand and Shun. Ceramic knives are also pretty

Once you've mastered your produce shopping routine, dive into stocking your pantry. Bulk bins and shelves lined with superfoods will become a happy haven. (See page 85 for more details on my favorite superfood finds.)

## When to Buy Organic

When talking produce, one of the most common questions I get is: How important is it to buy organic?

Easy: buy organic as much as possible. This allows you to maximize your nutrient intake, avoid common pesticides and toxins, and support farmers who are doing their best to choose healthier methods for the planet and for us. Organic fruits and vegetables taste better and have consistently been shown to contain higher amounts of vitamins and minerals than nonorganic produce.

The problem, of course, is that organics are generally more expensive and not universally available (although on both accounts things are changing for the better). If you've got the money and the access, go 100 percent organic. But if you're like most people, that may be difficult. The good news is you don't have to be perfect in order to eat safer and healthier. That's because when it comes to pesticides and other toxins, not all produce is created equal. Some absorb more of the bad stuff during conventional farming, while others absorb very little. If you buy organic for just the few worst offenders while allowing nonorganic for the least,

you'll be in good shape without breaking the bank. My friends at the Environmental Working Group created the incredibly helpful "Dirty Dozen" and "Clean Fifteen" lists. Think of these must-haves as your shopping road map: memorize them, print them out, download their app—whatever it takes for you to use them. Keep in mind that they get updated yearly, so you'll want to check back in for the most current recommendations.

If you can't shop organic, period, that's okay, too. The most important thing is that you juice and blend those fruits and veggies! If you're juicing nonorganic produce (like cucumbers, carrots, or apples), just be sure to peel them first and wash them thoroughly before running them through your juicer. For more tips on washing produce, check out page 66.

## Tips for Saving Money

While we're on the topic of grocery shopping, let's talk budgeting. As you already know, all of the gorgeous, organic produce you plan to stock your kitchen with can add up. But it's definitely less expensive than doctors' bills, excessive medications for lifestyle-related ailments, missed days at work due to poopy health, and so on. It'll take a little extra time and effort, but if you'd like to make juices and smoothies less of a strain on your purse strings, try adopting a few of these helpful habits. (You'll also be

## THE DIRTY DOZEN

1 APPLES

2 PEACHES

3 NECTARINES

4 STRAWBERRIES

5 GRAPES

6 CELERY

7 SPINACH

8 SWEET BELL PEPPERS

9 CUCUMBERS

10 CHERRY TOMATOES

11 SNAP PEAS (IMPORTED)

12 POTATOES

13 *RUNNER UP:* HOT PEPPERS

14 *RUNNER UP:* KALE / COLLARD GREENS

## THE CLEAN FIFTEEN

1 AVOCADOS

2 SWEET CORN

3 PINEAPPLE

4 CABBAGE

5 SWEET PEAS (FROZEN)

6 ONIONS

7 ASPARAGUS

8 MANGOES

9 PAPAYAS

10 KIWI

11 EGGPLANT

12 GRAPEFRUIT

13 CANTALOUPE

14 CAULIFLOWER

15 SWEET POTATOES

doing Mama Earth a solid when you follow some of these suggestions.)

**SUPPORT YOUR LOCAL FARMERS' MARKETS.** Farmers' market produce isn't always cheap, but farmers will often offer specials on fruits and vegetables that are at the height of freshness. You may be able to get your haggle on at your local market, too—particularly at the end of the day when farmers don't want to pack up what didn't sell.

**JOIN A CSA.** Here's how it works: in the winter, you buy an advance share of the produce that a particular farmer or co-op plans to grow for the year ahead. When the crop starts coming, you swing by the farm (or a set pick-up location) and grab your share on a designated day. It's amazing how many bags of fresh greens you'll start to see in early spring—in fact, you may not be able to make it through all of your produce, in which case you can go halvsies with a friend.

A CSA share usually runs about $400 to $500 a year—sometimes less if you choose a smaller package. This sounds like a lot of money, but once you start collecting sexy sacks of fabulous produce each week, I guarantee you'll realize it's a huge bargain. Don't just take my word for it, though; crunch some numbers and see if it makes sense for you. CSAs are also a great way to discover new, exotic produce since you don't always have a choice of what's in the weekly haul.

SHOP ONLINE. Another great way to save moolah is to shop online. Stores like Vitacost and Thrive Market have become virtual health hubs that offer great products at deep discounts. These companies also offer free or reasonable shipping prices. In the case of Thrive Market, there's an annual membership fee (similar to Costco) but with one big difference: when you buy a membership, Thrive gives one away to a low-income family! While these stores don't offer vegetables (yet) they're a great place to get bulk staples like superfoods and healthy sweeteners at near wholesale prices.

BUILD ON WHAT YOU HAVE. Examine your fridge and cupboards. What can you build on? What needs to be used up? If you have viable produce at home, then don't run out to purchase more just yet. Think about what fabulous recipes you can create with what you have.

MAKE PLANS. To avoid running low on fruits and vegetables, try to plan out your week of beverages before you shop. This will help you to resist sneaky impulse buys, shop more efficiently, and save money. Divide your grocery list into staples (the fruits and veggies you just can't live without), seasonal picks (stuff that's not necessarily a staple, but which you want to take advantage of by season, like apples in the fall or peaches in the summer), and splurges (superfood goodies). Think about what you can afford, and do some trimming from your list, if necessary. For a free downloadable meal plan, go to kriscarr.com. I love making helpful stuff for you!

WASTE NOT, WANT NOT. Leftover broccoli stems from last night's stir-fry? They're great in a juice! Got half an avocado from lunch? Let that be the base of your next creamy green smoothie. Fruit and veggie odds and ends are ideal for juicing and blending, so take advantage. One of the biggest causes of waste is buying too much, only to find a slimy mystery bag in the bottom of the crisper a week later. Live food has a short shelf life compared to those Twinkies, so plan wisely.

SAVVY SUBSTITUTIONS. If certain ingredients are weighing your budget down, look for more affordable alternatives. Raisins make a great substitute for pitted Medjool dates; sunflower seeds are cheaper than cashews, and they offer similar creaminess. Depending on the season, a particular type of green might be cheaper than the one that's called for in a recipe, so feel free to switch and swap. Check out the substitutions list on page 95 for help.

REVIEW THE DIRTY DOZEN AND THE CLEAN FIFTEEN. Check out the Environmental Working Group's lists (printed on page 60) to determine your priorities for organic purchases. Choose organic for produce on the Dirty Dozen list and conventional for the Clean Fifteen (or for most fruits and veggies that have thick skins).

LET YOUR GARDEN GROW. If you have space, start your own vegetable and herb garden. A two-dollar packet of mixed lettuce seeds will support your juicing habit for months. Even if you live in a major metropolis, you can still invest in growing your own greens and herbs. When I lived in Brooklyn, NY, I grew sprouts in my bathroom and herbs on my windowsill. Today I have a raised-bed garden in my backyard, and each year I learn more and more about how to grow our food (AKA not kill my plants).

There are many great books (and websites) on gardening. Here are a few of my favorite reads: *The Vegetable Gardener's Bible* by Edward C. Smith, *Grow Organic* by Doug Oster and Jessica Walliser, *Starter Vegetable Gardens* by Barbara Pleasant, and *You Grow Girl* by Gayla Trail (perfect for the urban gal or guy). Also, check out fourseasonfarm. com. Greening your thumb is easier than you think!

KEEP YOUR PRODUCE FRESH LONGER. Review the Ingredients Section (page 65) for proper storage tips that will extend the life of your fruits and veggies. When recommended, use those Debbie Meyer GreenBags I've been raving about like an excited lunatic.

BUY USED, OR BARTER. Buying a new juicer or blender may not be in your budget right now, but what about a used one?

The only caveat is that most of these used machines are not returnable and have no warranty—so ask for a test run before you buy. As I mentioned earlier, some companies do offer cheaper, reconditioned machines with warranties. Craigslist or eBay, not to mention your friends and family, might also have an affordable gently used model. Perhaps you can barter with those great boots that are too small for you. A purrrfect swap! Amazon, eBay, and Bed Bath & Beyond offer sales and competitive prices, so take time to do your homework.

SKIP THE FANCY ADD-ONS. Instead of buying every trendy superfood that can fit in a blender, try one at a time and slowly build up your arsenal. Go ahead and splurge once in a while, but if you're looking for somewhere to cut corners, skip the exotic stuff and focus your energy (and funds) on quality produce.

TIGHTEN YOUR BELT IN OTHER AREAS. Do you cruise Target looking for sparkly tanning lotions, huggable hangers, "deals," and "cheap" gadgets? I know you do, because I do. If you think about it, I'm sure you've got some frivolous spending habits you could lose. Redistribute your funds. Use them where they matter most. Remember that every single green drink you create is an investment in your quality of life—now and always.

# 4

# SPOTLIGHT ON INGREDIENTS

Ahhh . . . the bountiful harvest. In this chapter, I'm going to open your purdy peepers to the ingredients that are the juicing and blending all-stars.

This info is divided into three sections: leafy greens, fruits and veggies, and superfood boosts. This definitive guide will show you how to pick, prep, and store your favorite foods. You'll also learn about the top nutrients and benefits of these plant gems—plus how to choose a substitute for those you'd rather avoid. Before we jump in, let's talk about how to clean these cuties.

# Washing and Cleaning Produce

Before you put your gorgeous produce into the juicer or blender and down your glamorous gullet, it's important to be sure that you've washed off bacteria, debris, sand, and dirt. Most resources suggest that fresh produce should be washed under tap water for at least 30 seconds to remove dirt and microorganisms. (Rinsing is better than soaking, because sinks and soak containers can harbor little critters!) Use a scrub brush for hard surfaces like beets, carrots, and cucumbers. For leafies and other delicates, rinse and rub gently. Nonorganic produce should always be washed to help remove pesticide residues. Food scientists have found that using water is just as effective as standard fruit and vegetable washes.

Depending on your health needs and circumstances, there are a few other cleaning options you can use:

**Flash Pasteurization:** This is an aggressive but reliable means of making sure that produce ends up squeaky clean and bacteria-free—which may be important to those who are immunocompromised (for example, if you're going through a treatment such as chemotherapy). Bring a pot of water to boil, then dip your veggies in it for no more than 20 seconds. Fragile greens need only about 5 seconds. This procedure will kill most, if not all, the germs while keeping nutrients intact.

**Hydrogen Peroxide Vegetable Soak:** This option reliably removes bacteria and is another suitable method for those who may have weakened immune systems. However, it's very important that you follow precautions or serious injury can occur. Food-grade hydrogen peroxide is typically available in a 35 percent solution. This is a very strong concentration and can burn skin on contact. It must be diluted with water down to 3 percent before using to clean your food. Do an online search for help with proper dilution.

**White Vinegar Vegetable Soak:** You can also try white vinegar for cleaning your produce. Fill a large bowl with water and add about a half cup of vinegar. Let your veggies (or fruits) sit for about 20 minutes before rinsing and using.

# Spotlight on Greens

Say hello to your new BFF, greens! These babies are nutrient-dense stunners. The more you embrace them, the happier and healthier your body will be.

## Arugula

**SELECTION:** Choose arugula with long, firm, bright green leaves without holes, tears, or bright yellow edges.

**STORAGE:** Store in the vegetable drawer of the fridge for 2 to 3 days.

**PREPARATION FOR USE:** Wash thoroughly to remove dirt and grit.

**TOP NUTRIENTS:** carotenoids beta-carotene, lutein, and zeaxanthin, vitamin K, sulforaphane, chlorophyll

**HEALTH BENEFITS:** promotes healthy eyes and skin, fights cancer, boosts immunity, builds healthy bones, helps in blood clotting, detoxifies the body, builds and purifies blood, revitalizes cells, combats inflammation

## Collards

**SELECTION:** Leaves should be firm and deep green with no signs of wilting or yellowing.

**STORAGE:** Unwashed greens can be stored in the fridge in a plastic bag with as much air removed as possible for 4 to 6 days.

**PREPARATION FOR USE:** Wash leaves individually, making sure to remove all dirt and grit. Bunch or roll up the leaves before running them through your juicer, taking care to follow them with a more watery fruit or vegetable (apples, cucumber, celery, carrot, pineapple, etc.). Most leaves are a suitable size for blending, but larger leaves can be sliced in half if necessary.

**TOP NUTRIENTS:** carotenoid beta-carotene, vitamin C, vitamin K, calcium, choline

**HEALTH BENEFITS:** promotes healthy eyes and skin, fights cancer, boosts immunity, acts as an antioxidant, builds healthy bones, helps in blood clotting, helps keep blood pressure down, boosts memory, may help lower cholesterol

## Dandelion greens

**SELECTION:** Leaves should be flat, crisp, unwilted, and bright green without any yellowing.

**STORAGE:** Unwashed greens can be stored in a plastic bag in the low-moisture veggie drawer in the fridge for up to 5 days.

**PREPARATION FOR USE:** Wash thoroughly to remove all dirt and grit.

**TOP NUTRIENTS:** carotenoids lutein and zeaxanthin, vitamin C, vitamin K, calcium

**HEALTH BENEFITS:** promotes healthy eyes and skin, fights cancer, boosts immunity, combats inflammation, acts as an antioxidant, builds healthy bones, helps in blood clotting, helps keep blood pressure down, detoxifies the body

## Kale

**SELECTION**: Leaves should be unwilted, small to medium in size for best tenderness, deep green in color with no yellowing or browning, and stems should be moist.

**STORAGE**: Store unwashed in a plastic bag in the fridge with as much air removed as possible to maintain freshness for up to 5 days. The longer kale sits in the fridge, the more bitter it will become.

**PREPARATION FOR USE**: Wash leaves individually to remove all dirt and grit. If your leaves are very large, you can juice them one by one. For most bunches of kale (any variety—curly, purple, or lacinato), you can juice three or four leaves at a time.

**TOP NUTRIENTS**: carotenoids beta-carotene and lutein, vitamin C, vitamin K, calcium, copper, isothiocyanates

**HEALTH BENEFITS**: promotes healthy eyes and skin, fights cancer, boosts immunity, acts as an antioxidant, builds healthy bones, helps keep blood pressure down, supports proper growth, aids in energy production, acts as an antimicrobial, detoxifies the body

## Romaine

**SELECTION**: The head should be closely

bunched and leaves should be crisp without any slimy or dark spots, or any browning or wilting.

**STORAGE**: Wash and dry leaves with a paper towel and then store in a plastic bag in the fridge for up to a week.

**PREPARATION FOR USE**: Separate leaves and submerge them in a bowl of water, moving them around to help remove dirt and grit, and then rinse them individually. Run the leaves through your juicer several at a time, or break them up before blending.

**TOP NUTRIENTS**: carotenoid beta-carotene, folic acid, vitamin K

**HEALTH BENEFITS**: promotes healthy eyes and skin, fights cancer, boosts immunity, combats inflammation, supports healthy cells and genetic material, builds healthy bones, helps in blood clotting

## Spinach

**SELECTION**: Choose crisp, green bunches with no evidence of insect damage.

**STORAGE**: Wrap loosely in a damp paper towel and store in the fridge in a plastic bag for 3 to 5 days.

**PREPARATION FOR USE**: Submerge leaves in a bowl of water, moving them around to help remove dirt and grit. Rinse the leaves. For best results when juicing, bunch spinach up before running it through your juicer.

**TOP NUTRIENTS**: carotenoids beta-carotene, lutein, and zeaxanthin, folic acid, vitamin K, copper, iron, manganese

**HEALTH BENEFITS**: promotes healthy eyes and skin, fights cancer, boosts immunity, combats inflammation, supports healthy cells and genetic material, builds healthy bones, helps in blood clotting, supports proper growth, aids in energy production, improves oxygen transport throughout the body, promotes the healthy metabolism of fats and carbohydrates

# Fruit and Vegetable All-Stars

Meet my favorite fruits and vegetables! They're bound to perk you up and add yum to your recipes.

## Swiss chard

**SELECTION**: Leaves should be vivid green with no signs of wilting or browning. Stalks should be crisp and undamaged.

**STORAGE**: Store, unwashed, in an airtight plastic bag in the fridge for up to 5 days. Extra chard can be blanched and frozen for 1 month.

**PREPARATION FOR USE**: Separate chard leaves from the bunch and wash individually, taking care to rinse the stems well. (This is where dirt and grit can collect.) Bunch the leaves up before running them through your juicer, taking care to follow them with a more watery fruit or vegetable (apples, cucumber, celery, carrot, pineapple, etc.).

**TOP NUTRIENTS**: carotenoids beta-carotene, lutein, and zeaxanthin, vitamin C, vitamin K, copper, magnesium, quercetin, kaempferol

**HEALTH BENEFITS**: promotes healthy eyes and skin, fights cancer, boosts immunity, acts as an antioxidant, builds healthy bones, helps in blood clotting, supports proper growth, aids in energy production, increases muscle relaxation for improved blood flow, promotes heart health

## Apples

**SELECTION**: Fruit should be firm, colorful, and not at all wrinkled or yielding to pressure. Brown spots are okay and rarely affect taste.

**STORAGE**: Store in perforated plastic bag in refrigerator for up to 4 months.

**PREPARATION FOR USE**: Wash and core apples, removing the seeds. For juicing, be sure to cut them into pieces that are small enough to fit through the juicer mouth (to help avoid juicing traffic jams). If your apples aren't organic, peel them.

**TOP NUTRIENTS**: vitamin C, anthocyanins (in red-skinned apples)

**HEALTH BENEFITS**: acts as an antioxidant, combats inflammation, fights cancer, prevents heart disease

## Avocados

**SELECTION**: Ripe avocados are slightly soft when pressed, and dark in color; firm

avocados will ripen in 3 to 5 days. Avoid ones with sunken spots, cracks, or dull color.

**STORAGE:** Use ripe avocados immediately or store them in the fridge for up to 1 week. Placing unripe avocados in a paper bag may speed up ripening by 1 day, or they can be placed in the fridge to slow down the ripening process. Leftover avocados can be stored in the fridge with the pit, sprinkled with lemon juice, and wrapped in plastic wrap to avoid browning.

**PREPARATION FOR USE:** Cut your avocado in half lengthwise and use a small spoon to scoop out the pit. Scoop out flesh with a larger spoon before adding it to smoothies.

**TOP NUTRIENTS:** vitamin B5 (pantothenic acid), folic acid, vitamin E, vitamin K, potassium

**HEALTH BENEFITS:** detoxifies the liver, supports healthy cells and genetic material, acts as an antioxidant, builds healthy bones, helps in blood clotting, helps keep blood pressure down

## USING AVOCADO

Avocado (AKA nature's butter) is a magical smoothie muse; more than any other ingredient, it'll add a creamy, almost fluffy texture to your blends. Be careful not to add too much, though, or your blend will resemble a pudding more than a smoothie (which, on second thought, sounds divine). I find that half of a small Hass avocado is a perfect amount. Avocado pairs particularly well with tropical fruits, berries, and greens.

**STORAGE:** Ripen bananas at room temp. Peel and freeze ripe or overripe (all brown) bananas in a plastic bag for smoothies for up to 6 months.

**PREPARATION FOR USE:** Peel and freeze before blending if possible.

**TOP NUTRIENTS:** vitamin B6, vitamin C, potassium, manganese

**HEALTH BENEFITS:** maintains sodium-potassium balance in your body, promotes red blood cell production, acts as an antioxidant, helps keep blood pressure down, promotes the healthy metabolism of fats and carbohydrates

## Bananas

**SELECTION:** Choose bananas that are firm, vibrant yellow, and without bruises. They taste the sweetest when they have small brown spots.

## Basil

**SELECTION:** Choose organic (nonirradiated), fresh leaves that are vibrant and deep green without dark spots.

**STORAGE:** Store wrapped in a damp paper towel for up to 5 days in the fridge. It can be chopped and frozen in an airtight container and kept for up to 6 months.

**PREPARATION FOR USE:** Submerge the basil—stems and leaves both—in a bowl of water and swish it around to release all dirt. Shake it dry before running it through your juicer or adding it to smoothies. If your herbs seem spiffy, then it's fine to simply rinse them well before using.

**TOP NUTRIENTS:** vitamin K, manganese, flavonoids, volatile oils

**HEALTH BENEFITS:** builds healthy bones, helps in blood clotting, promotes the healthy metabolism of fats and carbohydrates, combats inflammation

## Beets

**SELECTION:** Choose small- or medium-sized beets with smooth skin and deep color. Avoid beets that have spots or bruises, or are shriveled or flabby.

**STORAGE:** Store in a plastic bag in the fridge for up to 3 weeks.

**PREPARATION FOR USE:** Trim the tough ends off, then wash the beets and cut them into pieces that will fit into the mouth of your juicer.

**TOP NUTRIENTS:** folic acid, manganese, potassium, betalains

**HEALTH BENEFITS:** supports healthy cells and genetic material, promotes the healthy metabolism of fats and carbohydrates, helps keep blood pressure down, acts as a strong antioxidant

## Bell peppers

**SELECTION:** Choose peppers that are heavy and have brightly colored, tight skin. Stems should be green and fresh looking. Avoid peppers with blemishes, spots, or wrinkles.

**STORAGE:** Store in a plastic bag in the fridge for up to 5 days.

**PREPARATION FOR USE:** Remove the stem of the pepper by cutting around it with a paring knife and gingerly pulling it out. This will remove most of the seeds. Wash and quarter the pepper before juicing or blending.

**TOP NUTRIENTS:** carotenoids alpha-carotene, beta-carotene, cryptoxanthin, lutein, and zeaxanthin, vitamin C, vitamin B6, flavonoids

**HEALTH BENEFITS:** promotes healthy eyes and skin, fights cancer, boosts immunity, acts as an antioxidant, maintains sodium-potassium balance in the body, promotes red blood cell production, combats inflammation

## Blackberries

**SELECTION:** Choose berries that are shiny and very dark in color, not bruised or leaking.

**STORAGE:** Store unwashed in the fridge for 3 to 5 days and wash right before eating. Freeze extras in a plastic bag for up to 1 month.

**PREPARATION FOR USE:** Wash well before freezing, blending, or juicing.

## STORING HALVSIES

Sometimes a recipe calls for only half of an ingredient (cucumber, banana, avocado, whatever). To keep your halves fresh, you can store them in an airtight container in the fridge with a small piece of damp paper towel covering the cut surface. (This works especially well for cucumbers.)

If you're storing avocado halves, sprinkle the cut half with lemon juice prior to storing. You can store your lemon halves and avocado halves in the same container, too. If you have a half and a quarter left (a lot of my recipes call for ¼ avocado), then be sure to press a cut side of the quarter against the half. And always keep pits in your avocado halves if possible; they'll help to keep the fruit fresher, longer!

**TOP NUTRIENTS:** vitamin C, anthocyanins, gallic acid

**HEALTH BENEFITS:** acts as an antioxidant, combats inflammation, works as an antidiarrheal, acts as an antibacterial

## Blueberries

**SELECTION:** Berries should be a bit firm, plump, unshriveled, with a silver-white coating.

**STORAGE:** Store in a sealed container in the refrigerator for up to 10 days, or in plastic bags in the freezer for up to 6 months.

**PREPARATION FOR USE:** Wash well before freezing, blending, or juicing.

**TOP NUTRIENTS:** vitamin K, manganese, anthocyanins, quercetin, kaempferol, resveratrol

**HEALTH BENEFITS:** builds healthy bones, helps in blood clotting, promotes the healthy metabolism of fats and carbohydrates, prevents heart disease, combats inflammation

# Broccoli

**SELECTION:** Choose broccoli with compact floret clusters that are uniform in color with no yellowing, bruising, or yellow flowers throughout. Stems should be firm without slimy spots. Leaves (if present) should be crisp, not wilted.

**STORAGE:** Store, unwashed, in an airtight plastic bag in the fridge for up to 10 days.

**PREPARATION FOR USE:** Wash and cut broccoli or broccoli stems into pieces that will fit through the mouth of your juicer.

**TOP NUTRIENTS:** folic acid, vitamin C, vitamin K, chromium, sulforaphane, indoles

**HEALTH BENEFITS:** supports healthy cells and genetic material, acts as an antioxidant, builds healthy bones, helps in blood clotting, may enhance insulin performance, detoxifies the body, combats inflammation, eliminates excess estrogen and carcinogens, provides protection against cervical and breast cancers, protects the liver, and helps detoxify the body

# Cabbage (Green/Red)

**SELECTION:** Heads should be firm and dense with crisp, shiny leaves free of bruising or blemishes. Only a few leaves should be loose. Precut cabbage pieces have less vitamin C.

**STORAGE:** Store whole heads in a plastic bag in the fridge for up to 2 weeks. Pieces of cabbage can be stored in an airtight container or bag for up to 3 days.

**PREPARATION FOR USE:** Wash and slice cabbage head into pieces that will fit into your juicer; it's typically easiest to cut a head of cabbage into quarters, then continue halving them until you have properly sized pieces.

**TOP NUTRIENTS:** vitamin C, vitamin K, anthocyanins (in red cabbage), glucosinolates, isothiocyanates

**HEALTH BENEFITS:** acts as an antioxidant, builds healthy bones, helps in blood clotting, combats inflammation, fights cancer, prevents heart disease, protects against chemical carcinogens, acts as an antimicrobial

# Carrots

**SELECTION:** Choose firm and deep orange carrots without cracks, and ones that aren't limp or rubbery. Larger carrots are generally sweeter.

**STORAGE:** Carrots will last longer if they retain as much of their moisture as possible. Store wrapped in paper towels in an airtight bag in the fridge for up to 2 weeks.

**PREPARATION FOR USE:** Wash carrots and trim off the tops. If they aren't organic, peel them.

**TOP NUTRIENTS:** carotenoids beta-carotene and lutein, biotin

**HEALTH BENEFITS:** promotes healthy eyes, fights cancer, boosts immunity, strengthens hair, nails, and skin, may help lower cholesterol and improve blood sugar control

## Celery

**SELECTION**: Choose crisp celery that snaps easily. Stalks shouldn't splay out.

**STORAGE**: Store in an airtight plastic bag in the fridge for 5 to 7 days.

**PREPARATION FOR USE**: Wash your stalks before juicing. Juice the entire stalk (leafy head included). If the bottoms of the stalks are sandy or gritty, trim them before juicing.

**TOP NUTRIENTS**: vitamin K, acetylenics, coumarins, phthalides

**HEALTH BENEFITS**: builds healthy bones, helps in blood clotting, fights cancer and has tumor-shrinking potential, improves white blood cell activity, may lower high blood pressure

## Cherries

**SELECTION**: Choose shiny, dark maroon or black cherries with fresh-looking stems.

**STORAGE**: Store in a sealed container in the refrigerator for up to 10 days.

**PREPARATION FOR USE**: Rinse and use a paring knife to remove pits.

**TOP NUTRIENTS**: carotenoids beta-carotene, lutein, and zeaxanthin, vitamin C, anthocyanins, quercetin

**HEALTH BENEFITS**: promotes healthy eyes and skin, fights cancer, boosts immunity, acts as an antioxidant, combats inflammation, prevents heart disease

## Cilantro

**SELECTION**: Leaves should be firm, crisp, and vibrant green without yellow or brown spots.

**STORAGE**: Wrap leaves in a damp paper towel and store in a plastic bag. Store in the fridge for up to 3 days.

**PREPARATION FOR USE**: Cilantro can be juiced or blended whole—stems and leaves. Most fresh herbs do contain some grit, so I recommend submerging them in a bowl of water and swishing them around to release all dirt. Shake them dry before using them. If your herbs seem spiffy, it's fine to simply rinse them well before using.

**TOP NUTRIENTS**: vitamin K, quercetin, volatile oils

**HEALTH BENEFITS**: builds healthy bones, helps in blood clotting, acts as an antioxidant, combats inflammation, promotes heart health

## Coconuts, young Thai

**SELECTION**: Choose young coconuts that are heavy for their size and so full of liquid that you can't hear it sloshing around when shaken.

**STORAGE**: Store unopened coconuts at room temp for up to 2 months. Portions of opened up coconuts can be stored in a plastic bag or container in the fridge for up to 7 days.

## OPENING A YOUNG THAI COCONUT

The meat of young Thai coconuts is rich in fiber and fatty acids, while the coconut water contains electrolytes that may help boost our immune systems. It's also creamy and delicious, and it will add a characteristically tropical taste to your smoothie blends. Finally, it's a great fat source for those who have almond or avocado allergies.

Opening Thai coconuts is a bit daunting, but once you get the hang of it, you'll be hacking yours open like a pro. First, shave off some of the excess husk from the pointy top of the coconut. Next, tap gently around the top of the coconut using a kitchen cleaver or a large chef's knife with a heavy bottom. If you hear a spot that sounds particularly hollow, that's a good place to make your first cut.

Keeping your non-cleaver hand firmly tucked behind your back, use the cleaver or knife to strike the coconut tip where it seems to be hollow-sounding. Continue hacking around the top of the coconut until you've essentially cut out a little "cap" around the coconut tip (4 to 5 hacks should do it). Pull off the cap and use a spoon to scrape out the tender meat. It will last, stored in an airtight container in your fridge, for about seven days.

Does all of this sound like too much work? The good news is that at least one brand, Exotic Superfoods, now sells frozen young Thai coconut meat. You can find it at select health-food stores, or check out http://www.exoticsuperfoods.com for more information.

**PREPARATION FOR USE:** See directions for opening a young Thai coconut (above).

**TOP NUTRIENTS:** copper, iron, manganese, potassium

**HEALTH BENEFITS:** supports proper growth, aids in energy production, improves oxygen transport throughout the body, promotes the healthy metabolism of fats and carbohydrates, helps keep blood pressure down

## Cucumbers

**SELECTION:** Choose cucumbers that are green to dark green, firm, and rounded at the edges. Avoid ones with sunken spots, yellowing, or puffiness.

**STORAGE:** Store in the fridge for 7 to 10 days. Wrap portions of cucumber in plastic wrap or store in an airtight container to prevent drying out.

**PREPARATION FOR USE:** Wash and cut into pieces that will fit through the mouth of your juicer. If your cucumbers aren't organic, peel them before juicing. If you're blending the cucumber, cut it into halves or quarters before adding it to your blender.

**TOP NUTRIENTS:** vitamin K, molybdenum, cucurbitacins, lignans

**HEALTH BENEFITS:** builds healthy bones, helps in blood clotting, helps in the metabolism of RNA and DNA, may block cancer cell development and survival, performs as an antiviral, combats inflammation, acts as an antibacterial, reduces the risk of cancer and heart disease

## Daikon

**SELECTION**: The skin should be firm, shiny, and smooth without bruises or cracks.

**STORAGE**: Wrap tightly in plastic and refrigerate for up to 3 days.

**PREPARATION FOR USE**: Trim the tops and leaves off the radishes and wash thoroughly.

**TOP NUTRIENTS**: vitamin C, copper

**HEALTH BENEFITS**: acts as an antioxidant, supports proper growth, aids in energy production

## Dates

**SELECTION**: Dates should be shiny, uniformly colored, and unbroken.

**STORAGE**: Store in an airtight container at room temp for up to 6 months, or in the fridge for up to 1 year.

**PREPARATION FOR USE**: Remove the pits from dates before blending.

**TOP NUTRIENTS**: manganese, potassium, polyphenols

**HEALTH BENEFITS**: promotes the healthy metabolism of fats and carbohydrates,

helps keep blood pressure down, acts as an antioxidant

## Fennel

**SELECTION**: Choose fennel with lean, firm, solid, green bulbs with no signs of browning or bruising. The stalks should be green, straight, and not splayed out, and have a mild licorice aroma.

**STORAGE**: Store in the fridge crisper for up to 4 days.

**PREPARATION FOR USE**: Wash and cut each bulb into quarters before blending or juicing.

**TOP NUTRIENTS**: vitamin C, molybdenum, potassium, terpene beta-sitosterol

**HEALTH BENEFITS**: acts as an antioxidant, helps keep blood pressure down, aids in digestion

## Ginger

**SELECTION**: Choose fresh ginger that is smooth, firm, and mold-free.

**STORAGE**: Unpeeled, fresh ginger will last in the fridge for up to 3 weeks and in the freezer for up to 6 months.

**PREPARATION FOR USE**: Cut off the desired-size piece for your recipe and remove the skin with a paring knife or by running the edge of a spoon over it from top to bottom. If you don't have a high-speed blender, you may want to mince your ginger before blending, or grate it with a microplane grater, as it can be tough to blend up. Powdered ginger is also a nice option for blending; you should use about half the quantity of fresh ginger that the recipe calls for.

**TOP NUTRIENTS**: gingerols

**HEALTH BENEFITS**: combats inflammation, aids in digestion

## Grapefruit

**SELECTION**: Fruit should be heavy for its size and the peel may have mild blemishes; these won't affect the taste or quality.

**STORAGE**: Grapefruits are juicier at room temp, so store them in a fruit bowl for up to 1 week and then in the fridge for up to 3 weeks.

**PREPARATION FOR USE**: Peel the grapefruit (or use a paring knife to cut off the skin) and cut into pieces that will fit your juicer. The pith contains antioxidants, so it's fine if some of it remains on the fruit, although too much will lend bitterness to your blend. Seeds can be left in the fruit for juicing or blending with a high-speed blender. If you're using a conventional blender, be sure to remove seeds from the fruit.

**TOP NUTRIENTS**: carotenoid lycopene, vitamin C, flavonoid naringenin

**HEALTH BENEFITS**: helps prevent prostate cancer, acts as an antioxidant, combats inflammation

## Grapes

**SELECTION**: Grapes should be plump, wrinkle-free, and firmly attached to fresh-looking stems. They should be uniform in color with the area connected to the stem the same color as the rest of the grape: green grapes should be yellowish, red grapes should be mostly red.

**STORAGE**: Store, unwashed, in an airtight container in the refrigerator for up to 5 days.

**PREPARATION FOR USE**: Remove grapes from the stems and wash.

**TOP NUTRIENTS**: vitamin C, vitamin K, copper, catechins, resveratrol

**HEALTH BENEFITS**: acts as an antioxidant, builds healthy bones, helps in blood clotting, supports proper growth, aids in energy production, prevents heart disease, combats inflammation

## Honeydew

**SELECTION**: Honeydew melons should be creamy white with a dull luster. Shiny melons are underripe. They should sound hollow when tapped with the palm of the hand, and the end where the vine was attached should be slightly soft and have a mildly sweet aroma.

**STORAGE**: Store ripe, uncut melon in the fridge for up to 5 days. Store ripe, cut melon halves with seeds, wrapped in plastic in the fridge for up to 3 days.

**PREPARATION FOR USE:** Cut your melon into quarters and use a paring knife to remove skin. Be sure to scoop out the seeds.

**TOP NUTRIENTS:** vitamin C, potassium

**HEALTH BENEFITS:** acts as an antioxidant, helps keep blood pressure down

## Jalapeño

**SELECTION:** Peppers should be brilliant in color with firm, glossy skin. Avoid those that are wrinkled or have soft spots.

**STORAGE:** Wrap in paper towels or in a paper bag and store in the fridge for up to 1 week.

**PREPARATION FOR USE:** Wash pepper, cut a desired piece, and use. Jalapeños are very (holy hotness) spicy, so be sure not to touch sensitive skin or rub eyes after you've handled them.

**TOP NUTRIENT:** vitamin C

**HEALTH BENEFITS:** acts as an antioxidant

## Kiwifruit

**SELECTION:** Choose kiwifruit that is plump, unwrinkled, and unblemished. It is ripe when it yields slightly to pressure.

**STORAGE:** Fruit can be ripened at room temp in a paper bag with an apple or banana to speed up the process. Once ripe, store it in a sealed container in the refrigerator for up to 2 weeks.

**PREPARATION FOR USE:** Peel before juicing or blending.

**TOP NUTRIENTS:** vitamin C, vitamin K, potassium

**HEALTH BENEFITS:** acts as an antioxidant, builds healthy bones, helps in blood clotting, helps keep blood pressure down

## Lemons

**SELECTION:** Choose fruit that is deep yellow, shiny, and heavy for its size. Avoid fruit that is wrinkled or dull in color.

**STORAGE:** Store at room temperature out of sunlight for up to 1 week and in the vegetable crisper of the fridge for up to 1 month.

**PREPARATION FOR USE:** Peel lemons and cut them to fit into your juicer. It's fine to leave the pith on. If using lemon juice in smoothies, squeeze and measure fresh juice and add it to your smoothie blend.

**TOP NUTRIENTS:** vitamin C, limonoids

**HEALTH BENEFITS:** acts as an antioxidant, fights cancer of the mouth, skin, lung, breast, stomach, and colon

## PEELING CITRUS

There are many ways to peel citrus fruits (including lemons, limes, grapefruits, and oranges) for juices and smoothies. If you have a method that works for you, then it's fine to keep using it. I personally like to use a paring knife to slice off the ends of the citrus fruit. I then set the citrus fruit down on one of its two peeled ends, and I use my knife to cut the skin off in vertical strips, moving from the top of the fruit to the bottom.

It's not necessary to seed lemons, limes, oranges, or grapefruit for fresh juices. For smoothies, you'll need to remove seeds if you're using a conventional blender. If you're using a high-speed blender, it's okay to throw the fruit in, seeds and all!

Final note: though bitter to taste, the pith of an orange contains as much vitamin C as the fruit itself, so it's fine if some of it remains on the fruit before juicing or blending.

## Limes

**SELECTION:** Choose plump limes that are heavy for their size with a deep green, glossy peel. Avoid ones that have a lot of brown on the peel, as they may have a moldy taste.

**STORAGE:** Store at room temperature out of sunlight for up to 1 week and in the vegetable crisper of the fridge for up to 1 month.

**PREPARATION FOR USE:** Peel limes and cut them to fit into your juicer. It's fine to leave the pith on. If using lime juice in smoothies, squeeze and measure fresh juice and add it to your smoothie blend.

**TOP NUTRIENTS:** vitamin C, limonoids

**HEALTH BENEFITS:** acts as an antioxidant, fights cancer of the mouth, skin, lung, breast, stomach, and colon

## Mangoes

**SELECTION:** Choose slightly firm mangoes with red, green, and orange skin and a slightly sweet aroma. Mangoes are ripe when they are slightly soft.

**STORAGE:** Store on the counter until ripe. Speed up ripening in a paper bag. Store in the fridge for up to 2 days once ripe.

**PREPARATION FOR USE:** Peel the mango and cut slices around the large pit.

**TOP NUTRIENTS:** Beta-carotene, vitamin C

**HEALTH BENEFITS:** promotes healthy eyes and skin, fights cancer, boosts immunity, acts as an antioxidant

## Mint

**SELECTION:** Choose mint with bright green, vibrant leaves. Avoid mint with yellowing or dark spots.

**STORAGE:** Store in the fridge wrapped loosely in a damp paper towel and in a plastic bag for up to 1 week.

**PREPARATION FOR USE:** Mint can be juiced or blended whole—stems and leaves both. Most fresh herbs do contain some grit, though, so I recommend submerging them in a bowl of water and swishing them around to release all dirt. Shake them dry before using them. If your herbs seem spiffy, then it's fine to simply rinse them well before using.

**TOP NUTRIENT:** terpene perillyl alcohol

**HEALTH BENEFITS:** aids in digestion

## Oranges

**SELECTION:** Choose oranges that are firm and heavy for their size. They don't need to be uniform in color; brown spots or green color are not a bad thing. Avoid fruit with soft spots. Smaller oranges will be juicier.

**STORAGE:** Store in the fridge for up to 2 weeks.

**PREPARATION FOR USE:** Peel the orange (or use a paring knife to cut off the skin) and cut it into pieces that will fit in your juicer. The pith contains antioxidants, so it's fine if some of it remains on the fruit. Seeds can be left in the fruit for juicing or blending with a high-speed blender. If you're using a conventional blender, be sure to remove seeds before blending.

**TOP NUTRIENTS:** vitamin C, folic acid, tangeretin, nobiletin

**HEALTH BENEFITS:** acts as an antioxidant, supports healthy cells and genetic material, combats inflammation, prevents heart disease, protects against Alzheimer's and Parkinson's disease

## Parsley

**SELECTION:** Choose bunches with bright green, crisp leaves. Avoid those with wilting or yellowing leaves.

**STORAGE:** Store in the fridge in a plastic bag for up to 1 week.

**PREPARATION FOR USE:** Parsley can be juiced or blended whole—stems and leaves both. Most fresh herbs do contain some grit, so I recommend submerging them in a bowl of water and swishing them around to release all dirt. Shake them dry before using them. If your herbs seem spiffy, then it's fine to simply rinse them well before using.

**TOP NUTRIENTS:** carotenoids beta-carotene, lutein, and zeaxanthin, vitamin C, vitamin K, iron, chlorophyll, luteolin

**HEALTH BENEFITS:** promotes healthy eyes and skin, fights cancer, boosts immunity, acts as an antioxidant, builds healthy bones, helps in blood clotting, improves oxygen transport throughout the body, builds and purifies blood, revitalizes cells, combats inflammation, prevents tumor growth

## Peaches

**SELECTION:** Ripe peaches yield slightly to pressure and shouldn't have soft spots or bruises. Undercolor should be creamy yellow or gold. The red "blush" of the peach isn't an indication of ripeness.

**STORAGE:** Firm peaches will ripen at room temp in 2 to 3 days or 1 to 2 days in a paper bag with an apple, pear, or banana. Refrigerated ripe peaches will last 5 to 7 days.

**PREPARATION FOR USE:** Wash, cut in half, and remove the pit before using. If the peaches are organic, skin can be left on. If peaches aren't organic, use a paring knife to peel them.

**TOP NUTRIENTS:** vitamin C, potassium, anthocyanins

**HEALTH BENEFITS:** acts as an antioxidant, helps keep blood pressure down, combats inflammation, fights cancer, prevents heart disease

## Pears

**SELECTION:** Choose firm pears without bruises and let them ripen for 2 to 3 days. Brown speckled patches are okay and may indicate a sweeter, more intense flavor.

**STORAGE:** Speed up ripening by placing them in a paper bag. Once ripe, refrigerate for up to 3 days. Store away from other strong-smelling fruits or vegetables as they will absorb those aromas.

**PREPARATION FOR USE:** Wash and core pears, removing the seeds. For juicing, be sure to cut them into pieces that are small enough to fit through the juicer mouth. If your pears aren't organic, then try to peel them.

**TOP NUTRIENTS:** vitamin C, vitamin K

**HEALTH BENEFITS:** acts as an antioxidant, helps build healthy bones, helps in blood clotting

## Pineapple

**SELECTION**: Pineapple should be heavy for its size and free of soft spots or dark "eyes," and have a pleasant aroma. Pineapple stops ripening as soon as it is picked, but it will get softer and juicier after a few days at room temperature.

**STORAGE**: Store uncut pineapple in a plastic bag in the refrigerator for up to 5 days. Store cut pineapple in some of its own juice in a sealed container for up to 3 days.

**PREPARATION FOR USE**: Cut off the top of the fruit and slice the pineapple into quarters. Cut out the woody core of the fruit and then use a paring knife to remove the skin.

**TOP NUTRIENTS**: vitamin C, manganese, bromelain

**HEALTH BENEFITS**: acts as an antioxidant, promotes the healthy metabolism of fats and carbohydrates, combats inflammation, slows the growth of tumor cells

## Raspberries

**SELECTION**: Choose plump, tender berries that are uniform in color. Avoid leaking or moldy berries.

**STORAGE**: Store in the fridge in a non-airtight shallow container for 3 to 5 days and wash only right before eating. Freeze extras in a plastic bag for up to 1 month.

**PREPARATION FOR USE**: Wash well before freezing, blending, or juicing.

**TOP NUTRIENTS**: vitamin C, manganese, anthocyanins, ellagic acid, hydroxycinnamic acids, resveratrol

**HEALTH BENEFITS**: acts as an antioxidant, promotes the healthy metabolism of fats and carbohydrates, combats inflammation, acts as an antimicrobial, may cause cancer cell death, prevents heart disease

## Strawberries

**SELECTION**: Choose berries that have a shiny, deep red color and attached green caps. Avoid those that are shriveled or moldy. Plan to eat strawberries within 3 days.

**STORAGE**: Remove soft or moldy strawberries from the group before storing the rest in an airtight container in the fridge. They should remain fresh for up to 3 days. Only wash right before eating.

**PREPARATION FOR USE**: Wash well before freezing, blending, or juicing.

**TOP NUTRIENTS**: vitamin C, manganese, anthocyanins, ellagic acid, hydroxycinnamic acids, resveratrol

**HEALTH BENEFITS**: acts as an antioxidant, promotes the healthy metabolism of fats and carbohydrates, combats inflammation, acts as an antimicrobial, may cause cancer cell death, prevents heart disease

## Tarragon

**SELECTION:** Choose fresh tarragon that has bright green leaves that are not wilted, limp, or have dry brown or yellow areas.

**STORAGE:** Store in a sealed bag in the refrigerator crisper away from tomatoes, bananas, and peppers for up to 5 days.

**PREPARATION FOR USE:** Tarragon can be juiced or blended whole—stems and leaves. Most fresh herbs do contain some grit, so I recommend submerging them in a bowl of water and swishing them around to release the dirt. Shake them dry before using them. If your herbs seem spiffy, it's fine to simply rinse them well before using.

**TOP NUTRIENT:** eugenol

**HEALTH BENEFITS:** stimulates the appetite, acts as an antioxidant

## Watermelon

**SELECTION:** Choose an uncut watermelon that is firm, shiny but slightly dulled on top, and heavy for its size (water content increases with ripening). The ground spot (where the melon was in contact with the soil) on a fully ripened watermelon will be creamy yellow, not light green or white. Cut watermelon should be deep pink in color.

**STORAGE:** Whole melons are ideally stored in a basement area where the temperature is cooler than room temp and warmer than the fridge (50 to 60 degrees Fahrenheit). Whole melons shouldn't be stored near ethylene-producing fruits like passion fruit, peaches, pears, apples, or papaya, as they may ripen too quickly. Once cut, store in an airtight container in the fridge for up to 3 days.

**PREPARATION FOR USE:** Cut watermelon into large wedges. Use a sharp knife to remove the rind and seeds, and cut watermelon pieces into large chunks.

**TOP NUTRIENTS:** lycopene, vitamin C

**HEALTH BENEFITS:** helps prevent prostate cancer, acts as an antioxidant

# Superfood Boosts

"Superfood" is a big buzzword these days, and it can be hard to figure out what the term really means. Think of it this way: a superfood is any ingredient that happens to be incredibly rich in micronutrients (vitamins, minerals, and phytochemicals). As you'll see, many nuts and seeds (including coconut and pumpkin seeds) qualify as superfoods, as do a bunch of commonly used spices, like cinnamon.

There are a couple of specialty ingredients—many indigenous to South and Central America—that are labeled as superfoods because their nutrient profiles are so incredibly unique. These include maca, a libido-boosting tuber that's usually sold in powder form, and acai, an antioxidant-rich, deep purple berry that's native to Trinidad and northern regions of South America. These ingredients aren't essential for a healthy lifestyle, but they can be fun to experiment with, and while they're sometimes on the pricier side, fortunately, a little goes a long way.

## Acai

**SELECTION:** Choose frozen acai puree (such as in a smoothie pack) that is unsweetened, organic, non-GMO, and free of preservatives or colorings.

**STORAGE:** Store in the freezer as long as package indicates (sometimes up to 5 years). Once thawed, store puree in the fridge and use within 2 days.

**PREPARATION FOR USE:** Acai is typically sold in frozen packs that can be added to smoothies. You can use half a pack or a whole pack at a time, depending on the recipe in question. Just be sure to purchase an unsweetened variety, per the above, as the sweetened acai packs can be very high in sugar.

**TOP NUTRIENTS:** vitamin C, calcium, anthocyanins, beta-sitosterol, essential fatty acids

**HEALTH BENEFITS:** acts as an antioxidant, combats inflammation, fights cancer, promotes heart health, lowers LDL (bad) cholesterol and increases HDL (good) cholesterol

## Almonds

**SELECTION:** Choose raw almonds that are uniform in color, and not shriveled or limp. If buying in bulk, be sure inventory is turned over frequently. They should smell sweet and nutty, not sharp and bitter (those are rancid).

**STORAGE:** Store in an airtight container in a cool, dry place away from sunlight. Almonds stored in an airtight container in the fridge will last for several months.

**PREPARATION FOR USE:** Raw almonds should be soaked for 8 hours (or overnight) and rinsed before blending into smoothies or nut milks. See my tips on page 275 for more.

**TOP NUTRIENTS:** vitamin E, biotin, copper, manganese

**HEALTH BENEFITS:** acts as an antioxidant, strengthens hair, nails, and skin, may help lower cholesterol and improve blood sugar control, supports proper growth, aids in energy production, promotes the healthy metabolism of fats and carbohydrates

## Aloe vera

**SELECTION:** Choose bottled juice that is organic, unflavored, in a BPA-free bottle, and free of sugar and preservatives. (I recommend the Lily of the Desert, Fruit of the Earth, or Nature's Way brands.)

**STORAGE:** Store according to bottle instructions. Bottled aloe vera juice can typically be stored in a cool, dark place for quite some time. Once opened, juice should be refrigerated and will typically last up to 2 months.

**PREPARATION FOR USE:** Simply measure liquid aloe vera from the bottle before adding to juices or smoothies.

**TOP NUTRIENTS:** lignins, saponins, essential fatty acids

**HEALTH BENEFITS:** reduces the risk of cancer and heart disease, enhances nutrient absorption, fights cancer, detoxifies the body, aids in digestion

# Brazil nuts

**SELECTION:** Choose raw Brazil nuts that are whole, brown, heavy, and not shriveled or damaged. If buying in bulk, be sure inventory is turned over frequently. They should smell sweet and nutty, not sharp and bitter (those are rancid).

**STORAGE:** Store Brazil nuts in an airtight container a cool, dry place away from sunlight. Storing them in the fridge will increase their shelf life and help prevent them from going rancid.

**PREPARATION FOR USE:** Brazil nuts should be soaked for 4 hours and rinsed prior to blending in smoothies or nut milk (see my tips on page 275 for more). The nuts have a relatively soft, "buttery" texture, so if you have a high-speed blender, you can skip the soaking step if you forget.

**TOP NUTRIENTS:** copper, magnesium, phosphorus, selenium, essential fatty acids

**HEALTH BENEFITS:** supports proper growth, aids in energy production, increases muscle relaxation for improved blood flow, supports healthy bone formation, digestion, and hormone balance, acts as an antioxidant, promotes heart health, lowers LDL (bad) cholesterol, and increases HDL (good) cholesterol

# Cacao / Cacao nibs

**SELECTION:** Choose organic.

**STORAGE:** Store nibs in an airtight container or bag with excess air squeezed out. Store at room temp or below in a dark area without sunlight exposure or moisture.

**PREPARATION FOR USE:** Measure your quantity of cacao nibs before blending and add the nibs directly to your blender. Cacao nibs take a few moments to blend completely. Cacao powder, on the other hand, will blend quickly and easily. It's more potent in taste than regular cocoa powder, so remember that a little will go a long way.

**TOP NUTRIENTS:** iron, catechins, anthocyanins

**HEALTH BENEFITS:** improves oxygen transport throughout the body, acts as an antioxidant, combats inflammation, acts as an antimicrobial, fights cancer, prevents heart disease

# Cashews

**SELECTION:** Choose raw cashews with a sweet, nutty flavor.

**STORAGE:** Store in an airtight container in the fridge for up to 6 months or in the freezer for up to 1 year.

**PREPARATION FOR USE:** Soak cashews for between 2 and 4 hours and rinse before blending into nut milks or smoothies (see my tips on page 275 for more).

**TOP NUTRIENTS**: copper, magnesium, manganese, phosphorus, zinc

**HEALTH BENEFITS**: supports proper growth, aids in energy production, increases muscle relaxation for improved blood flow, promotes the healthy metabolism of fats and carbohydrates, supports healthy bone formation, digestion, and hormone balance, aids in healthy enzyme activity, boosts immunity

## Cayenne

**SELECTION**: Choose organic powder.

**STORAGE**: Store in a tightly sealed glass jar out of sunlight for up to 6 months.

**PREPARATION FOR USE**: Add a small quantity of cayenne powder to smoothies or juices. Cayenne is very hot, so be mindful.

**TOP NUTRIENTS**: carotenoid beta-carotene, capsaicin

**HEALTH BENEFITS**: promotes healthy eyes and skin, fights cancer, boosts immunity, reduces pain, promotes heart health, acts as a nasal decongestant

## Chia seeds

**SELECTION**: Choose organic chia seeds that don't stick together, or organic chia powder.

**STORAGE**: Store in an airtight container or bag at room temp for up to 1 year. Ground chia seeds can be stored in an airtight container in the fridge for up to 1 month.

**PREPARATION FOR USE**: Chia seeds can be added directly to a high-speed blender. If you're using a regular blender, try grinding your chia seeds in a coffee grinder, spice mill, or food processor prior to adding it to smoothies (you can use a 1:1 ratio for replacing whole chia with ground chia).

**TOP NUTRIENTS**: calcium, iron, protein, essential fatty acids

**HEALTH BENEFITS**: builds healthy bones, helps keep blood pressure down, improves oxygen transport throughout the body, promotes heart health, lowers LDL (bad) cholesterol, and increases HDL (good) cholesterol

## Cinnamon

**SELECTION**: Sticks or powder should have a sweet smell indicating that it's fresh.

**STORAGE**: Store in a tightly sealed glass container in a cool, dark, dry place. Powder will last up to 6 months, sticks will last up to 1 year.

**PREPARATION FOR USE**: If you're using cinnamon sticks, grate the desired amount of cinnamon powder prior to adding it to a regular blender (you can also use a spice mill). If you have a high-speed blender, you can add pieces of cinnamon stick directly to the blender, though it may be easier to use ground cinnamon for measurement purposes.

**TOP NUTRIENTS**: manganese, cinnamic acid

**HEALTH BENEFITS:** promotes the healthy metabolism of fats and carbohydrates, may improve insulin sensitivity

## Coconut oil

**SELECTION:** Choose refined coconut oil for a less coconutty flavor, but ensure it doesn't include hydrogenated or partially hydrogenated fat. Choose raw, unrefined, virgin, or extra virgin coconut oil for a more coconutty flavor.

**STORAGE:** Store in the pantry for up to 2 years.

**PREPARATION FOR USE:** Coconut oil is solid below room temperature and liquid above. You can add either the solid or liquid form to your smoothies. If you don't have a high-speed blender, it may be easiest to melt it beforehand if it's in the solid form.

**TOP NUTRIENTS:** medium chain triglycerides (MCTs)

**HEALTH BENEFITS:** boosts energy

## Coconut water

**SELECTION:** If buying commercial, choose coconut water with few preservatives.

**STORAGE:** Store fresh coconut water in the fridge for up to 3 days or freeze for up to

### FLAX SEEDS

Flax seeds add mood and brain-boosting omega-3 fatty acids, fiber, and cancer-fighting lignans to smoothies. If you have a high-speed blender, you can blend flax seeds up whole in your smoothies, but I prefer to use flax seeds that are already ground. You can purchase whole flax seeds at any health-food or grocery store and then grind them in a food processor, coffee grinder, spice mill, or high-speed blender, or you can save yourself a little time and purchase the seeds preground.

1 month. Store commercial coconut water according to package instructions.

**PREPARATION FOR USE:** Add coconut water directly to smoothies or juices according to recipe instructions.

**TOP NUTRIENTS:** potassium, magnesium, cytokinins

**HEALTH BENEFITS:** helps keep blood pressure down, increases muscle relaxation for improved blood flow, performs as an antiviral, acts as an antibacterial

## Flax seeds / Flax meal (ground flax seeds)

**SELECTION:** Choose either ground or whole flax seeds that are clear of any moisture. Make sure if buying in bulk that bins are turned over frequently.

**STORAGE:** Ground flax seeds can be stored in an airtight container in the fridge for up to 4 months. Whole flax seeds can be stored in an airtight container in a cool, dry, dark place for up to 12 months, or up to 2 years in the fridge.

**PREPARATION FOR USE:** See sidebar on page 90 for more information.

**TOP NUTRIENTS:** lignans, essential fatty acids

**HEALTH BENEFITS:** fights cancer, promotes heart health, lowers LDL (bad) cholesterol, and increases HDL (good) cholesterol

## Goji berries

**SELECTION:** Choose dried berries that are sun-dried without preservatives. They should be a brilliant red and not too hard or leathery.

**STORAGE:** Store in a sealed container in a dark place at room temp for up to 1 year, or in a sealed container in the fridge for up to 2 years.

**PREPARATION FOR USE:** Goji berries have a tough texture, so you may wish to soak them before blending, even if you have a high-speed blender. Soak them in warm water for 30 minutes and drain before adding them to smoothies.

**TOP NUTRIENTS:** carotenoids beta-carotene and zeaxanthin, vitamin C, iron, copper, selenium

**HEALTH BENEFITS:** promotes healthy eyes and skin, fights cancer, boosts immunity, acts as an antioxidant, improves oxygen

transport throughout the body, supports proper growth, aids in energy production

## Hemp seeds

**SELECTION:** Choose raw seeds which are uniform in color, or hemp hearts (shelled hemp seeds) which show no signs of moisture or mold.

**STORAGE:** Store seeds or hearts in a sealed container in the fridge for up to 12 months.

**PREPARATION FOR USE:** Hemp hearts or shelled hemp seeds can be blended directly into smoothies or nut milks.

**TOP NUTRIENTS:** protein, essential fatty acids

**HEALTH BENEFITS:** builds healthy cells and tissues, promotes heart health, lowers LDL (bad) cholesterol, and increases HDL (good) cholesterol

## Maca

**SELECTION:** Choose organic, raw powder.

**STORAGE:** Store in a cool, dark, dry place (no refrigeration needed) for 6 months.

**PREPARATION FOR USE:** Can be added directly in specified amounts to smoothies.

**TOP NUTRIENTS:** vitamin C, copper, iron, glucosinolates

**HEALTH BENEFITS:** acts as an antioxidant, supports proper growth, aids in energy

## SUPERFOOD SIDEKICKS

The superfoods in this list don't simply have to be used when you're juicing or blending. Explore different nut milks and use them as a vehicle for your superfood ingredients. In the winter, I love to gently warm up a cup of almond or macadamia nut milk over the stove and add some spices (turmeric, ginger, cardamom) or superfoods (like maca, cacao, or matcha green tea). It's cozy and healthy!

production, improves oxygen transport throughout the body, protects against chemical carcinogens

## Macadamia nuts

**SELECTION:** Choose shelled nuts (raw if available) that are firm and shiny or oily.

**STORAGE:** Store shelled nuts in an airtight container in the fridge for 6 to 12 months.

**PREPARATION FOR USE:** Macadamia nuts should be soaked for between 2 and 4 hours and rinsed before blending into smoothies

or nut milks (see my tips on page 275 for more). The nuts have a relatively soft, "buttery" texture, so if you have a high-speed blender, you can skip the soaking step in a pinch.

**TOP NUTRIENTS:** vitamin B1, manganese, selenium

**HEALTH BENEFITS:** aids in the healthy breakdown of fats, protein, and carbohydrates, acts as an antioxidant

## Matcha green tea powder

**SELECTION:** Choose organic matcha powder that is unsweetened and bright green in color.

**STORAGE:** Store in a dark, cool, dry place, or in the fridge or freezer, but sealed tightly and away from strong smells, as it will take on neighboring aromas.

**PREPARATION FOR USE:** Can be added directly in specified amounts to smoothies. The powder can also be stirred by the quarter or half teaspoon into hot water for tea.

**TOP NUTRIENTS:** vitamin A, epigallocatechin gallate (EGCG)

**HEALTH BENEFITS:** promotes healthy eyes and skin, fights cancer, boosts immunity

## Pumpkin seeds

**SELECTION:** Choose organic, raw seeds. Avoid those with shriveling or any evidence of moisture.

**STORAGE:** Store in an airtight container in the fridge for up to 6 months.

**PREPARATION FOR USE:** Pumpkin seeds should be soaked for 8 hours (or overnight) and rinsed prior to blending into smoothies or seed milk. See my tips on page 275 for more.

**TOP NUTRIENTS:** copper, magnesium, manganese, phosphorus, zinc

**HEALTH BENEFITS:** supports proper growth, aids in energy production, increases muscle relaxation for improved blood flow, promotes the healthy metabolism of fats and carbohydrates, supports healthy bone formation, digestion, and hormone balance, aids in healthy enzyme activity, boosts immunity

## Raisins

**SELECTION:** Choose plump, moist raisins with wrinkles, not hard or too dried out.

**STORAGE:** Store raisins in a cool, dry place away from moisture and humidity. Once opened, store in the refrigerator in an airtight container to lengthen life and freshness.

**PREPARATION FOR USE:** If you have a high-speed blender, you can blend raisins directly into smoothies. If you don't, you should soak raisins in warm water for at least 30 minutes and drain the soak water before blending them.

**TOP NUTRIENTS:** iron, potassium, anthocyanins, resveratrol

**HEALTH BENEFITS:** improves oxygen transport throughout the body, helps keep blood pressure down, combats inflammation, fights cancer, prevents heart disease

## Sesame seeds / Tahini

**SELECTION:** Choose organic, raw seeds that have no evidence of moisture or a rancid smell. Choose organic, raw tahini.

**STORAGE:** Store sealed seeds and tahini in a cool, dark place until opened. Once opened, store in the refrigerator to prevent rancidity. Stir tahini before putting in the fridge, as it will be hard to stir once cold.

**PREPARATION FOR USE:** Raw sesame seeds should be soaked for 8 hours (or overnight) and rinsed prior to blending into smoothies or seed milk (see my tips on page 275 for more).

**TOP NUTRIENTS:** vitamin B1, calcium, copper, iron, magnesium, manganese, zinc

**HEALTH BENEFITS:** aids in the healthy breakdown of fats, protein, and carbohydrates, builds healthy bones, helps keep blood pressure down, supports proper growth, aids in energy production, improves oxygen transport throughout the body, increases muscle relaxation for improved blood flow, aids in healthy enzyme activity, boosts immunity

## Spirulina / Blue green algae

**SELECTION:** Choose organic powder.

**STORAGE:** Store in an airtight glass container in the refrigerator for up to 12 months.

**PREPARATION FOR USE:** Powdered blue green algae or spirulina can be added directly in specified amounts to smoothies.

**TOP NUTRIENTS:** carotenoid beta-carotene, copper, iron, chlorophyll, protein

**HEALTH BENEFITS:** promotes healthy eyes and skin, fights cancer, boosts immunity, supports proper growth, aids in energy production, improves oxygen transport throughout the body, builds and purifies blood, revitalizes cells, combats inflammation

## Turmeric root

**SELECTION:** Turmeric root looks similar to ginger, except it's smaller and has an orange hue. Make sure it's firm, smooth, and mold-free.

**STORAGE:** Store turmeric powder in a cool, dark, dry place for up to 6 months.

**PREPARATION FOR USE:** Cut off a suitable piece of turmeric for your recipe, and use a paring knife to remove the skin.

**TOP NUTRIENTS:** iron, manganese, volatile oils

**HEALTH BENEFITS:** improves oxygen transport throughout the body, promotes the healthy metabolism of fats and carbohydrates, combats inflammation

## Walnuts

**SELECTION**: If unshelled, choose nuts that are heavy and unblemished. If shelled, avoid rubbery or wrinkled nuts. They should smell fresh, not rancid.

**STORAGE**: Shelled and unshelled walnuts should be stored in an airtight container in the fridge for up to 6 months, or in the freezer for up to 1 year.

**PREPARATION FOR USE**: Walnuts should be soaked for 4 hours and rinsed prior to blending into smoothies or nut milks (see my tips on page 275 for more).

**TOP NUTRIENTS**: biotin, copper, essential fatty acids

**HEALTH BENEFITS**: strengthens hair, nails, and skin, may help lower cholesterol and improve blood sugar control, supports proper growth, aids in energy production, promotes heart health, lowers LDL (bad) cholesterol, and increases HDL (good) cholesterol

## Wheatgrass

**SELECTION**: Choose fresh or fresh-frozen wheatgrass juice.

**STORAGE**: Fresh wheatgrass juice should be consumed immediately, but can be frozen in a sealed ice cube tray or baby food tray for up to 7 days.

**PREPARATION FOR USE**: Wheatgrass juice can be added according to taste to smoothies or juices. Do not add blades of wheatgrass directly to your blender; you'll take in more nutrients and get a sweeter flavor if you add wheatgrass that has been juiced first.

**TOP NUTRIENTS**: carotenoid beta-carotene, vitamin E, phosphorous, chlorophyll

**HEALTH BENEFITS**: promotes healthy eyes and skin, fights cancer, boosts immunity, acts as an antioxidant, builds and purifies blood, revitalizes cells, combats inflammation, detoxifies the body

# Substitutions

Part of being a successful juice mixologist and smoothie master is knowing how to make savvy substitutions on the fly. This will help you work around your own likes/dislikes, manage food allergies, and roll with the punches when you happen to run out of an ingredient that's called for in a certain recipe. Here's a list of safe produce, nut/seed, and superfood swaps:

## Produce

**Apples**: Pears, grapes, kiwi

**Arugula**: Kale, dandelion greens, collard greens, spinach, watercress

**Avocado**: Young Thai coconut meat or banana for creaminess; nuts or nut butters to help replace fat

**Banana**: Mango, avocado, young Thai coconut meat, peaches

**Basil**: Mint

Beets: Carrots, radish, sweet potato

Blackberries: Blueberries, cherries, raspberries, strawberries

Blueberries: Blackberries, cherries, raspberries, strawberries

Broccoli: Cabbage

Cabbage: Broccoli

Cantaloupe: Honeydew, watermelon

Carrots: Sweet potato, beets, radish

Celery: Swiss chard, cucumber

Cherries: Blackberries, blueberries, raspberries, strawberries

Cilantro: Parsley

Coconut meat, young Thai: Avocado, banana

Coconut water: Water or watermelon juice

Collard greens: Kale, Swiss chard, spinach, dandelion greens, arugula

Cucumber: Celery, zucchini

Dandelion greens: Arugula, collard greens, kale, Swiss chard, spinach

Grapefruit: Orange

Grapes: Pear, apple, kiwi

Honeydew: Cantaloupe, watermelon

Kale: Arugula, collard greens, dandelion greens, Swiss chard, spinach

Kiwi: Apple, grapes, pear

Lemon: Lime

Lettuce (such as red leaf or Boston): Romaine

Lime: Lemon

Mango: Banana, peaches, nectarines, plums, pineapple

Maple syrup: Medjool dates

Medjool dates: Maple syrup

Mint: Basil

Nectarines: Peaches, plums, mango

Orange: Grapefruit, pineapple

Parsley: Cilantro

Peaches: Nectarines, plums, mango

Pear: Apple, kiwi, grapes

Pineapple: Orange, mango

Plums: Mango, nectarines, peaches

Radish: Sweet potato, beets, carrots

Raspberries: Blackberries, blueberries, cherries, strawberries

Romaine: Lettuce (such as red leaf or Boston)

Spinach: Arugula, collard greens, dandelion greens, kale, Swiss chard

Strawberries: Blackberries, blueberries, cherries, raspberries

Sweet potato: Beets, carrots, radish

Swiss chard: Celery, collard greens, kale, dandelion greens, spinach, arugula

Watercress: Arugula

Watermelon: Cantaloupe, honeydew

Zucchini: Cucumber

# Nuts & Seeds

**Almond butter:** Peanut butter, soy nut butter, cashew butter, sunflower seed butter, coconut butter

**Almonds:** Walnuts, pecans, Brazil nuts, cashews, peanuts

**Brazil nuts:** Almonds, cashews, macadamia nuts

**Cashews:** Macadamia nuts, pine nuts, Brazil nuts

**Coconut:** Cashews, macadamia nuts, Brazil nuts, avocado

**Hemp seeds:** Sunflower seeds, pumpkin seeds, sesame seeds

**Macadamia nuts:** Cashews, Brazil nuts

**Peanut butter:** Almond butter, soy nut butter, cashew butter, sunflower seed butter, coconut butter

**Peanuts:** Almonds

**Pecans:** Walnuts, almonds

**Pumpkin seeds:** Sunflower seeds, hemp seeds

**Sesame seeds:** Sunflower seeds, pumpkin seeds, hemp seeds

**Sunflower seeds:** Pumpkin seeds, hemp seeds, walnuts

**Walnuts:** Almonds, pecans, sunflower seeds

If you're allergic to most tree nuts, but you're not allergic to coconuts, try using coconut butter or young Thai coconut meat in smoothies in place of nuts or nut butter.

If you're allergic to tree nuts but not to seeds, try using sunflower seeds, pumpkin seeds, sesame seeds, or sunflower seed butter, pumpkin seed butter, or tahini in their place.

If you're allergic to all tree nuts and seeds, try using avocado in place of nuts to create creaminess in smoothies, rice or oat milk in place of almond (or other nut) milk, and soy nut butter in place of nut butters.

# Superfoods

**Cacao powder:** Carob powder

**Goji berries:** Raisins

**Hemp seeds:** Sunflower seeds, pumpkin seeds, sesame seeds

**Matcha green tea powder:** ¼ cup brewed and cooled green tea

**5**

# STAYING
# HOOKED

Almost anyone can get on the juice or smoothie bandwagon for a week or two. The real challenge is to turn this practice into a daily routine—like brushing your pearly choppers. Sure, you're busy, you've got places to be and things to do. But think about the big, bright picture. Making a juice or smoothie every day is one of the best investments you can make in your long-term health and fabulous future. If you're going to cut corners, don't do it here. Do you have time to feel like crap? Nope. Remember, we all have the same 24 hours in a day; invest them wisely, Yoda.

Fortunately, there are oodles of handy tips and tricks for sticking with your juicing and blending routine. These range from simple preparation to lifestyle practices. Here are some of my favorites:

KEEP YOUR APPLIANCES CLEAN AND VISIBLE. As I mentioned earlier, if your juicer is collecting dust in a cabinet (you know, that annoying one in the corner where you can't reach anything) or on the tippy-top shelf of your closet, then the chances of your making a green juice anytime soon are slim to none. If your blender hasn't seen sunlight since last year, then it'll be twice as hard to choose a green smoothie over chips.

Part of keeping your elixir habit in full force is having the equipment you need clean, visible, and at the ready.

PREP, PREP, PREP. Before you slip into your nightie and go to bed, wash and prep all of the ingredients for the next day. Place the ingredients in a bowl, cover it, stick it in the fridge, and set your juicer or blender up. In the morning, you'll have everything ready to go—and one less excuse not to get your green drink on.

KEEP A WELL-STOCKED FRIDGE. This is a universal tip for healthy living. If you don't have produce, you don't have juice or a smoothie—it's as simple as that. Over the weekend (or whenever you have time), make a list of the produce you'll need for the week. Take it with you when you do your weekly or biweekly grocery haul. If you work wacky hours and it makes your life easier to use a grocery delivery service like Fresh Direct, then go for it. But do whatever you can to keep fruits and veggies in your home.

TAKE IT ONE STEP AT A TIME. As you get started, remember to pace yourself. Integrate one smoothie or juice into your daily routine for a couple of weeks, and see where that takes you. You may become such an instant fan of these elixirs that you find yourself sipping them several times a day, but a single juice or smoothie each day is still a huge step toward a luminous life.

MAKE A SWAP. One of the easiest ways to slowly work juicing and blending into your life is to replace something else—something a little less awesome for you—with your groovy elixirs. Coffee fiend? Swap at least one of your cups of joe with a juice. Addicted to chips or pretzels? Try an afternoon smoothie instead. Sugar junkie? Juice is the best, most natural way to savor sweetness. Whatever your least wholesome habit is, see if you can't replace it with a beautiful, alkalizing beverage.

ADD BEFORE YOU REMOVE. This is one of my favorite tips for change—and for any wellness practice, not just juicing. So if even making a swap seems too dramatic, try this: Don't take anything away. Don't swap. Just add one healthy beverage at a time and go from there. When we increase the goodness in our lives, we naturally edge out what doesn't serve us. This also helps folks to feel less deprived.

ENLIST YOUR FAMILY. Teach your partner how to make smoothies. If your kids are old enough to operate a juicer or blender, show them how to use it—make discovery and creativity part of the fun. Let them whip up some combos (with supervision). When kids participate in making their own food, they are predisposed to trying and liking it. Having other folks in the family who can participate in your healthy habit will be a huge help to you as you incorporate this beautiful practice into your life.

FIND COMMUNITY. Whether it's exercising, meditating, or juicing, it's a proven fact that when people have support and are accountable to friends, they have an easier time sticking with healthy habits. Chances are there are folks just like you in your town. There are also many online communities and resources that champion this lifestyle—including my digital playgrounds! Come on over and introduce yourself. Kriscarr.com, Facebook, and Instagram are my favorite places to share recipes, tips, and inspiration.

# Self-Care Is Crazy Sexy

I never miss an opportunity to encourage you to love and care for your sweet self. Staying dedicated to your green drink practice isn't just about the beverages. Yes, green drinks are life-changing, but they're just one part of an interconnected, holistic lifestyle. Whole foods, exercise, and soul-nourishing

activities—they're all connected. And improving one area of your life helps improve the others. Staying motivated with the juicing and blending will be enhanced if you also keep an eye on the rest of your self-care regimen.

See your green drinks as a doorway, an entrance to profound shifts in the way you approach your relationship with food and well-being. As you experience these shifts, you might encounter some physical discomfort, depending on the quality of your current diet and how quickly and fully you immerse yourself in juicing and blending. If you decide to try my Three-Day Cleanse (page 291), for example, you may experience some headaches, crabbiness, digestive discomfort, or even a case of the sniffles as your body adjusts to new habits. Be patient, and know that these temporary symptoms are normal. They will pass like the gas coming out of . . . well, you get the idea.

The following self-care practices will not only help ease your transitional aches and pains, they will help dial up the benefits of feasting on alkaline-rich foods. They will also bring more balance and joy to your life. Most of them are focused on relaxation, nurturing the spirit, and taking care of your body even when you're not juicing or blending. Here are the ones that have made a wonderful difference for me:

SLEEP. You heard me. You can drink all of the nutrient-dense, alkaline juices and smoothies under the sun, but if you're not allowing your body to go into rest-and-recuperate mode, then you're still increasing your risk of disease (not to mention crankiness). Aim to get eight hours a night, and do your best not to get less than seven. Sleeping in a cool room with no light leaks really helps. So does turning your bedroom into a technology-free sanctuary, and skipping that afternoon latte.

MEDITATION. Meditation is to your mind and spirit what green juices are to your glorious bod: vital nourishment. If you've never meditated before, don't be intimidated. There are numerous resources to help. Pema Chödrön and Sharon Salzberg's books are fabulous; so is Jon Kabat-Zinn's *Wherever You Go, There You Are*. There are also many apps, podcasts, and videos available for beginners. Set aside a time of day for your meditation practice (ideally, in the morning). You don't have to become a monk; even 10 minutes will do.

GRATITUDE JOURNALING. The great thing about eating more mindfully is that the process can force us to slow down and notice the blessings all around us. Sometimes our thirst for quick fixes and instant results can skew our vision, making it difficult for us to acknowledge what's already miraculous. But when we practice giving thanks we get more to be thankful for. In addition, cleaning up our diets can clue us into the ways we've been numbing out with food, drink, and addictive substances. This is a good thing, because we can't transform what we don't see. So as you begin to connect with your body through these powerful drinks, start to think about what you're grateful for. Write it down. It doesn't have to be complicated, and you don't have to catalog everything.

MASSAGE. Lymphatic fluid is our partner in the fight against disease because it helps pull waste from our cells. Massage helps to keep

lymph circulating properly, which gives your body a hand in the cleansing and healing process.

EXERCISE. It's the perennial champion at the top of every list of what's good for you. Gentle forms of exercise like yoga or walking can be powerful healers and mood-lifters when practiced on a daily basis. Our bodies also love it when you shake it up and push them to their limits with short bursts of intense cardio. Spin class is great for that, but it can also come in the form of a quick, spaz-out dance break in the middle of the day. Nothing makes me happier than when I sweat my ass off. It boosts my heart rate, my happiness, and my derriere. Lastly, weight-bearing exercise is crucial for maintaining strong bones and joints. Ultimately, do what you can. The more you do it, the more your brain and body crave it.

INFRARED SAUNA OR STEAM BATH. Sweating in a sauna or steam bath helps you dump waste faster through the largest organ in your body—your skin. But along with all the toxins you're shedding, you're also losing a lot of water, so avoid dehydration by drinking as much water as possible before, during, and after your sauna session.

TAKE A BATH. Picture this: soothing music, pillar candles, cell phones off, and book pages crinkled by the steam from your decadent bath (*Fifty Shades of Grey* or *Farmer's Almanac*—whatever turns you on). Deep sigh. A warm bath with 1 to 2 cups of Epsom salts and some essential oils can help to soothe sore muscles, calm your nervous system, and improve circulation. Baths are an easy, inexpensive, and quick way to create a spa experience in the comfort of your own home.

**MAKE SPACE FOR FUN AND PLEASURE.** Without it, all the juices and smoothies in the world will do nada. Your diet is the fuel that keeps you going. Your soul, well, that's fueled by joy and space. I recommend several servings of smiles, multiple times per day.

# On the Road

One of the biggest things that can make you stray from these healthy habits is inconvenience—and one of the biggest inconveniences I've run into is travel. I travel a lot for work, so I've had to come up with some creative solutions for staying vibrant when living out of a suitcase. Whether you're sippin' vino in Napa, camping in the Rockies, or playing the slots in Vegas (personally, I prefer craps), you can still enjoy nourishing and energizing juices or smoothies, especially with my tried-and-true tips. Don't let travel be an excuse to drop your green habit!

**PERSONAL BLENDER.** If you travel frequently, then a compact and portable blender (like one of the fabulous Bullets) is a tremendous investment in your sustained health. When you get to your fancy destination, find the nearest grocery store, farmers' market, or health-food store, and pick up

some of your blending staples (nondairy milk, nut butter, bananas, and greens are mine). Whirl up your ingredients and enjoy a taste of home wherever you are. P.S.: Not all hotel rooms come equipped with a mini fridge, so make sure to call ahead. Keep in mind that many hotels will provide a fridge for a nominal fee. You could also bring along one of those small foldable coolers to keep your fruits, veggies, and any other perishables fresh overnight.

**LOCAL JUICE BARS.** If you're lucky enough to be near a juice bar (or a health-food store that sells fresh juices), skip the Starbucks latte and treat yourself to a juice or smoothie. No fuss, no mess, just effortless goodness in a glass without lifting a finger. Do a little Internet research before your trip and download some helpful phone apps for last-minute searches. My favorites are Yelp and VegOut and Happy Cow. Also, many Whole Foods have juice bars.

GREEN POWDER. Stash this in your carry-on and you're good to go. Green powders contain freeze-dried, dehydrated greens, and while they're not quite as tasty or fresh as the real thing, they're a handy substitute when you're bopping around the globe. Mix them with some filtered water, and voilà!

DON'T STRESS. So, you're worried you won't be able to do it all or keep up with all these helpful tips. Just do your best, dear one. It's not always possible or convenient to bring your new healthy habits with you as you jet-set around for work or play. Focus on what you can do. If you forgot your green powder and there's no way in heck you're going to be able to juice, can you sleep more? How about skipping the extra glass of wine in favor of water with lemon? What about a bath or a ten-minute meditation? Your body will be grateful for even the smallest gift of self-care—especially when you're in a foreign place and out of your normal routine.

# Getting Back on the Wagon

First and foremost, I don't believe in wagons, they're way too confining—and they're super old-fashioned—but there's a reason to talk about them. We all fall away from our good habits once in a while. No one is perfect.

And that's good; perfect is beige and boring anyway. So if you're struggling with fits and starts and all the beatings that go with them—dump that noise. That said, what happens when you've been juicing and blending like a champ, upgrading other areas of your life, and feeling frickin' fantastic, then all of a sudden you have a crappy day (or week or month)? Pick yourself up, dust yourself off, and move forward.

Now is a lovely time to have a heart-to-heart with the person in charge—you. Food can be a cozy emotional cork that keeps our issues stuffed in our tissues, making it easy to dowse our feelings in sugar and dunk 'em in a deep fryer till they're unrecognizable. The more present you are with your cravings, the more you'll be able to identify the feelings underneath them. The point is to take your self-care one day at a time and get to know yourself at the deepest level. Above all, be kind and patient. There's no need to slam on the gas and speed from 0 to 60. This is about slooowly and mindfully upgrading your life, not ruining it. So what if you started your day with a cup of coffee instead of a green juice? Enjoy the joe. No biggie. The stress of trying to be perfect can be just as acidic as the six-pack in your fridge. This is not about control or doing things "right," it's about an overall direction.

By reading this book, you've already committed to change and you're on the path to healthier living. I'm super proud of you, rock star.

# 6

# FAQs

In all of my years as a champion for wellness, I've gotten more questions about juicing and blending than any other topic. Finally, I have a chance to answer them all in one place. From digestive dilemmas to weight loss, here's my response to some of your most burning Q's.

## Can juicing or blending help me lose weight?

It sure can. Juices and smoothies are relatively low in calories, especially given how incredibly nutrient dense they are. They're the opposite of most processed food in America, which is full of calories but devoid of nutrients.

If you've been overdoing it on packaged snacks and drive-thru dinners, or struggling to get optimal nutrition in general, then learning how to create an uber-nourishing elixir could be the ticket to a leaner, more vibrant, healthier body.

It's important to keep in mind, though, that juices and smoothies will be what you want them to be. These aren't "diet drinks," and you don't have to greet them with the shudder you reserve for 100-calorie snack packs. The goal of these drinks is to bring you enhanced overall well-being.

If you're looking to lose weight in a healthy way, use these recipes to help you meet your goal. Try my suggestions for either making a swap or adding before removing (page 101). Both of these will help you enjoy the journey. Also remember, if weight loss is your goal, it may be helpful to focus on the less-sweet juices and smoothies in this book, or use my tips for reducing sugar in recipes (page 53), since sugar is associated with weight gain.

If you're just looking to maintain a weight you're already comfortable with, these drinks are a perfect part of the plan. Trying to gain weight? Smoothies are powerful vehicles for healthy fats and plant proteins that can bring you closer to your goal in a wholesome way.

## How many calories are in these drinks?

I'll be honest—I'm not a calorie counter. In my experience calorie counting focuses on restriction and deprivation rather than abundance. Plus, in spite of what you might have heard, healthy living isn't solely about "calories in" and "calories out." It's about the quality and value of the foods we put into our body. A 150-calorie juice will contain ten times the nutrition—vitamins, minerals, antioxidants—as a commercial snack bar with the same number of calories. (And it'll flood your body with hydration and clean energy, which is more than sugary and processed snacks can say.) More nutrition means we'll feel less prone to sugar cravings, more energized, and sharper. This in turn helps us make smart choices, again and again. There's a ripple effect when it comes to healthy food, and calories just don't tell the whole story.

## Juicing is a lot of work. Why can't I buy store-bought juices, like Naked or Odwalla, instead?

I'm often asked whether it's okay to skip all of this juicing business and purchase one of those handy store-bought juice blends. My answer? Meh . . . Many of the store-bought juices have unnaturally long shelf lives, typically achieved through pasteurization. Though pasteurization kills bacteria, it also depletes some of the micronutrients and enzymes. Plus, store-bought juices simply don't taste as yummy and fresh as homemade. More important, they're usually chock-full of added sugar. One of the biggest advantages of juicing at home is that you, sweet friend, get to control the quality, freshness, and sweetness of your juicy cocktails.

## Are juicing and blending safe and beneficial for cancer patients?

Juicing and blending can be a powerful way to invest in your own well-being when you're a cancer patient (AKA cancer thriver). There are two important things to keep in mind if you do incorporate juices or blends into your healing process: First, keep your drinks low in sugar. Sugar may encourage cancer growth, so for regular use you'll want to stick to fruits that are lower in sugar (see page 53 for more on this). To reduce your chances of having a blood sugar spike, sip your juices with some nuts or healthy fats like avocado. And, of course, fiber in smoothies will help, too. All these tips will help buffer the

absorption of sugar into your bloodstream, allowing you to include more of these overall health-boosting practices into your life. If you're taking a very strict approach to sugar, you can use my tips for eliminating or replacing fruit in your recipes (page 49) as well.

Second, if you're undergoing a treatment like chemotherapy, it's important to be vigilant about washing your produce to reduce your exposure to bacteria. Check out my instructions for fruit and vegetable cleaning methods (page 66).

## Are juicing and blending safe for pregnant women?

Juicing can be an ideal way to get more nutrition into your belly (and your baby's belly) when you're expecting a bundle of joy. (It's an especially good solution for sneaking in fruits and veggies when morning sickness has you shuddering at the thought of a salad.) Be sure to wash your produce carefully to reduce exposure to bacteria as much as possible. If you're buying from a juice bar, don't be afraid to ask about their cleaning, prep, and storage methods. Avoid commercial, unpasteurized juices for the duration of your pregnancy since you can't be sure how they're made, and consider running your juicy plans by your health-care provider before you get started. It's important not to undertake a juice fast while you're expecting, so if you are juicing, be sure that you're also getting plenty of delicious, alkaline, solid fare into your body, too!

Smoothies are also a great solution for adding more nutrition into your diet during pregnancy. Think about using recipes that are particularly nutrient dense, such as my pH Warriors (page 196) or Body Boosters (page 214). The latter group is full of extra iron, calcium, and protein.

## Are juices and smoothies safe for babies and kids?

Most experts agree that babies—especially those who are breastfeeding—don't need juices or smoothies in their diet (yet!). But juicing and blending are absolutely safe for kids, so long as you're mindful of portion size and sweetness. (Children don't need any help developing a sweet tooth.)

It's also important for your little ones to learn to *eat* their fruits and veggies, rather than just drink them, so serving your kids green drinks while also allowing them to develop a taste for solid fruits and vegetables is best. Experts say that babies 8 to 12 months old can have up to 4 to 6 ounces of green juice or smoothie per day, and that preschoolers between the ages of 1 and 3 can have up to 8 ounces of green juice or smoothie per day (the equivalent of one serving of fruit and one serving of vegetable). As your kids' recommended allowance of fruits and veggies increases, they can have more green drinks.

If you're worried about the sweetness, especially for preschoolers, you can dilute the juice or smoothie with water in a 1:1 ratio at first, and then ease the water out over time.

Before you incorporate juices or smoothies into your kids' diets, be sure to have a chat with your pediatrician about the particulars!

## Are juicing and blending safe for diabetics?

Juicing can be safe for diabetics, but it's important to keep your juices green, green, green. Even low-glycemic fruits may raise blood sugar, especially in the absence of fiber, so vegetable-only blends are often the safest bet. The juices in my "Cleansers" section (page 291) are, on average, the lowest in sugars, and can be reduced even further by swapping extra cucumber and/or celery in place of fruit. You can enhance their flavors with a splash of lemon, lime, or ginger. Check out my tips on lowering sugar in juice and smoothie recipes on page 53 for more guidance.

Depending on your situation, you may

be able to enjoy some low-glycemic fruits in moderation. If you do choose to consume fruits, you may wish to focus on smoothies more than juices, because the fiber in the smoothies helps ensure a slower absorption of sugar into your bloodstream. You can also choose to sip your juices—especially if they contain low-GI fruits—with a small amount of food that's rich in healthy fat or protein (for example, a handful of nuts). This will also help to buffer the absorption of sugar into your blood.

Once again, talk to your health-care provider before you embark on a juicing journey, and pay attention to how your body—and glucose levels, if you use a tester—responds.

## I have a digestive disease. Is juicing or blending better for me?

Juicing can be an important healing tool in the management of many digestive diseases, but one size doesn't fit all. If you're struggling with constipation, irritable bowel syndrome, or diverticulosis, then dietary fiber is your new BFF, and blending might be a better choice. If you have inflammatory bowel disease and are prone to flares, then juicing can be a gentle way to continue getting optimal nutrition without irritating your digestive tract. Chat with your health-care practitioner, and make a mutual decision about what's best for you.

## I've heard that too much raw kale is actually bad for you. Should I be worried?

When you're cautioned against going overboard with raw kale, you're probably being warned about one of two things. First, kale (along with all of its crucifer cousins such as broccoli, cauliflower, and cabbage) is what's considered a goitrogen—a food that can interfere with iodine uptake. In extreme cases of iodine deficiency, our thyroids can become enlarged, creating a swelling that's known as a goiter. In parts of the world where iodine intake is low, diets that are high in goitrogens may compound the effects of iodine deficiency. This is rarely a case in first-world countries, where most people get iodine through table or sea salt (or by eating sea vegetables!), so kale and other goitrogenic foods aren't something to worry about unless you have a preexisting thyroid condition. If you do, chat with your doctor before incorporating raw, cruciferous veggies into your juices or smoothies.

The other concern with juicing raw greens is that many of them, including spinach, chard, beet greens, and collards, contain naturally occurring compounds called oxalates. Oxalates can block our body's absorption of calcium and in some cases may contribute to kidney stone formation (although the evidence is inconclusive and other factors, such as a genetic predisposition, are stronger indicators). To be safe, people who are prone to kidney stone formation are usually advised to limit their consumption of oxalates. Since raw greens contain more oxalates than cooked greens, a little caution about juicing and blending them in excess is reasonable for those at risk of stones.

It's important to remember that, for most of us, the benefits of incorporating more greens into our diets significantly outweigh the potential pitfalls. As with so many health questions, moderation is everything. Rotate your greens and, when you're not juicing or blending, cook them for variety. Juices and smoothies are kick-ass health boosters, but they're one piece of a well-rounded diet.

## My juices and smoothies are: Just. Too. Green. Help!

Sister (and bro), this is a good problem to have. But if your juices bite you in the face with the taste of straight-up kale, then you may need to scale things back and add more watery veggies (like cucumber), plus a fruit. Zesty ingredients like lemon or ginger can mask the green while adding great flavor. Use our recipe collection as a guide.

## How do I make my juice less pulpy?

So you thought the whole point of juicing was to remove fiber, but you keep finding bits of pulp in your juice (and your teeth). Wassup with that?

Certain types of juicers (like the Breville Fountain Crush Slow Juicer) are actually designed to keep some pulp in the juice. So, it's just a sign that the machine's doing its job! Other juicers may let a few bits of pulp through every now and then, which is pretty normal, but it could also mean that you're trying to pack in more produce than your juicer can handle. Ease up, hotshot. If you love making lots of juice at once, be sure to stop halfway through, open up the machine, and clear the pulp from the parts. Then you can reassemble and continue.

You can also try straining your juice through a sieve or nut milk bag before sipping. Voilà! Problem solved.

## My juicer keeps jamming. What should I do?

Are you cutting your produce up into small enough pieces before juicing it? Even centrifugal juicers (which have nice, wide mouths) will jam if you stuff whole beets or apples in them. And remember that greens can give your juicer a hard time, so try to follow them up with something watery, like cucumber or apple (for more on this, see my tip on page 40). Most jams are caused when we're simply in too big of a rush. Take your time and don't force the plunger too hard. Let the machine do the work.

## What do I do with leftovers if I make too much juice?

Well, the best solution is to make smaller quantities. But I personally love making extra. As I mentioned earlier, you can store fresh juice in a mason jar and keep it cold until you're ready to drink more. If you have a masticating juicer or a twin gear juicer, it can last up to a few days. The more sugar content in a recipe, the sooner it will go south. Pay attention to the color of the juice when you make it. It loses its vibrancy as a way of telling you, "Better drink me soon or I'm plant food." Yes, you can feed slightly expired juice to your grateful plants.

You can also freeze juice. This is a great tip if your time is limited and you'd prefer to make a big batch all at once. I recommend freezing juices either in BPA-free plastic water bottles or in mason jars. If you use mason jars, be sure to leave some space up at the top (about an inch or so) because your juices will expand as they freeze. Frozen juice will last for about 10 days, but be sure to freeze the juice immediately after you prepare it, to ensure freshness.

## What should I do with my juice pulp?

So glad you asked! Don't despair, there's lots you can do with your pulp. Here are some of my favorite recycling ideas:

COMPOST. Juice pulp makes fabulous compost. How cool to think that we're using the scraps of our veggies to make our future veggie gardens grow! It's sorta like the "Circle of Life" song from *The Lion King*, but in your backyard.

CRACKERS. Juice pulp can be used to make delish, flour-free crackers. Check out the recipe on page 115 from my pal Gena Hamshaw, author of the blog and book *Choosing Raw*.

BURGERS. Want to infuse your homemade veggie burgers with even more fiber and texture? Check out the creative burger recipe on page 116, also from Gena Hamshaw.

If you do use your veggie juice pulp in a recipe, be sure to pick out tough, inedible seeds or other hard-to-digest bits before using, or else you'll end up with an impressive case of indigestion! Carrots, cucumber, leafy greens, and celery tend to make the best juice pulp.

## How do I make my smoothies thicker?

Take a chill pill with the almond milk or coconut water. In other words, add less liquid. A cup and a half of nut milk is usually enough. To rescue a watery blend, pour it back in the blender and add half a 'nana, ¼ avocado, or another thickening ingredient. Frozen fruits create thicker blends than the same amount of fresh fruits.

## How do I make my smoothies less thick?

This is an easy fix! If you're trying to pour your smoothie out of your blender and it won't budge, add a little more liquid. Start with a small amount—it doesn't take much to loosen it up. Add ¼ cup more nut milk, water, or coconut water at a time, and see if that does the trick.

# juice pulp crackers

Makes about 24 to 30 crackers

**2 heaping cups juice pulp (any veggies you like)**

**½ cup flax meal**

**3 tablespoons nama shoyu, tamari or (if you are gluten- and soy-free) coconut aminos**

**1 teaspoon coriander**

**½ teaspoon curry powder**

**Black pepper to taste (I'm generous with it)**

**¼ to ½ cup water**

1   Blend all ingredients except for the water in a food processor. Add water to the food processor in a thin stream till the mix is easy to spread but not watery. (The amount of water you'll need will vary based on how watery the pulp is.)

2   *If you have a food dehydrator:* Turn the "dough" out onto a Teflex-lined dehydrator sheet and spread it evenly (it should be about ¼-inch thick, or just less than that). Score into cracker shapes with a knife or a pizza cutter. Dehydrate the crackers at 115 degrees Fahrenheit for about 4 hours. Flip the sheet by putting another Teflex sheet over it, flipping it over, and then peeling off your original sheet. Dehydrate for another 4 to 5 hours, or until crackers are nice and crunchy (again, this time may vary based on how watery your pulp was).

   *If you don't have a food dehydrator:* Preheat your oven to 325 degrees Fahrenheit. Spread the "dough" thinly (about ¼-inch thick, or just less) on a parchment-lined baking sheet and score into cracker shapes with a knife or a pizza cutter. Place the sheet in the oven. Bake for 30 to 40 minutes, or until the crackers are crispy and dry, flipping them halfway through baking.

3   Store the crackers in an airtight container in a cool, dry place.

# juice pulp burgers

Makes 6 burgers

**1 tablespoon + 2 teaspoons olive oil, divided**

**1 cup finely chopped onion**

**1 clove garlic, minced**

**½ cup pumpkin seeds, raw or toasted**

**½ teaspoon salt**

**Black pepper to taste**

**1 cup vegetable juice pulp (carrot, kale, spinach, cucumber, beet, or celery all work well)**

**1 cup cooked chickpeas (navy, aduki, and cannellini beans work, too)**

**¼ cup cooked quinoa**

**1 teaspoon flax meal**

**1 tablespoon lemon juice**

**2 teaspoons chopped fresh thyme (optional)**

**1 teaspoon paprika (optional)**

**⅓ cup water**

1   Preheat your oven to 375 degrees Fahrenheit.

2   Heat 1 tablespoon of the olive oil in a skillet or sauté pan over medium heat. Add the onion and cook until the onion is tender and clear (5 to 7 minutes). Add the garlic and cook for another 30 seconds. Set aside.

3   Place the pumpkin seeds, salt, and pepper into the bowl of a food processor and process until they're coarsely ground. Add the juice pulp, chickpeas, quinoa, flax meal, lemon, thyme, and paprika, along with the water. Pulse the mixture continuously, until a sturdy dough has formed—sturdy enough to hold its shape, but moist enough that you can easily shape it into burgers (imagine a regular meatloaf or burger texture, even though this mixture is a little less uniform). If you need to add more water, do so by the tablespoon till the texture is right.

4   Shape the mixture into 6 uniform burger shapes. Place the burgers onto a parchment-lined baking sheet. Bake for 30 to 35 minutes, or until lightly browned, flipping them once halfway through. Leftover burgers will keep for 3 days in the fridge.

## How do I stop my blender from getting stuck when I'm trying to make smoothies?

There's nothing worse than blender interruption! But this is an easy problem to fix. If you have a high-speed blender (like a Vitamix), then use the tamp attachment to push ingredients down as you blend. If you're working with a conventional blender, then stop once or twice mid-blending to mix the ingredients up with a spatula or wooden spoon. Just be sure that the blender is OFF before doing this; bark chips ain't tasty. If the problem persists, you may need to add some liquid (see previous FAQ).

## I love smoothies, but I just can't handle the cold. Thoughts?

Are you suffering from brain freeze? Is there a blizzard outside your window, you're wearing three sweaters, and the mere thought of drinking something cold gives you hypothermia? My simple solution for this is to forgo frozen fruit and ice in recipes and use room temperature ingredients instead. It may also be helpful for you to start your day with more warming beverages and nourishing foods and enjoy your juices or smoothies later in the day after you've been more active. For a fabulous treat, try warming up your nut milks. Salud!

## I'm constipated. What should I do?

FIRST QUESTION: Are you getting enough plant fiber in your diet? You may be juicing up a storm, but if you're skimping on fiber the rest of the time or you've been replacing a lot of your meals with juices, then your body may be crying out for more fiber to fuel its digestive engines. If so, incorporate more whole grains (including wheat-free grains like amaranth, quinoa, and teff), big salads, cooked vegetables, and legumes into your diet.

SECOND QUESTION: Has irregularity been a nagging part of your life for a while now? Then getting more beneficial bacteria into your diet may be helpful. You can explore fermented foods (sauerkraut, kombucha, kefir, tempeh, fermented veggies, miso), or you can consider a probiotic supplement. Some of these have dairy byproducts in them, but a few brands, including Rainbow Life's ProbioActive, Renew Life's Ultimate Flora, and Garden of Life's RAW probiotics, offer maximum probiotic power without any funky fillers or dairy. Avoid taking probiotic supplements along with any hot liquids, as the heat can kill off the good bugs.

Magnesium can also be a helpful supplement for those who are dealing with mild constipation. (And as an added bonus, it can help with stress relief!) I like the Natural Calm brand, which comes in a powder form. You can mix it into water and sip it before bed—a soothing ritual for your soul and your gut.

Finally, it's important to remember that,

even if you're flooding your diet with fresh juices and smoothies, the rest of what you eat still matters. Too many animal products, processed foods, and other nonalkaline munchies will take a toll. Many processed foods are very dehydrating, high in sodium, and tough to digest. The more you limit these foods and maximize your consumption of water, the better you'll be able to keep things moving and grooving.

You can also consider a colonic (AKA colon hydrotherapy). Don't be afraid. It's just a little hose and some water up your butt. You've done tougher things in your life—guaranteed. There are different types of colonic hydrotherapy. The most gentle, safe, and effective kind is called a gravity colonic. It allows warm water to gently enter your colon while also allowing you to release waste. The entire process is clean and odorless, facilitated by a certified therapist who may even tell you interesting stories to pass the time (and the poo). Anyway, colonics aren't needed on a regular basis, but if you're backed up, they can be super helpful. Just be sure to find a practitioner who is well respected, certified, and takes the time to make you feel comfortable and confident.

## I'm making these drinks and I can't stop running to the bathroom. Help!

In all likelihood, one of two things is going on here. Either your body is responding to a flood of hydration from your juices, or it's dealing with an avalanche of fiber from your blends. In either case, diarrhea is your body's way of asking you to slow down (thank you very much). If you're consuming two or three juices or blends a day, try cutting back to one, and see how you feel. If you're blending up a ton of greens into your smoothies, try blending smaller amounts. Take it easy: juicing and blending is a lifelong love affair, not a race to the finish. If you see signs that tell you to slow down, heed them.

## I'm feeling sluggish. Am I doing something wrong?

As we transition away from some of our favorite pick-me-ups throughout the day (Frappuccinos, Red Bulls, candy bars) it's completely normal to feel temporary dips in energy, a withdrawal from the chemical-induced stimulation that's been standing in for real energy. The good news is that the more good stuff you drink, the less you'll

need or want your uppers. Give these juices and smoothies some time. They're not going to make your heart race (and pits sweat) the way a quad latte will. But if you make this a habit, they'll give your body the effortless and sustained energy it desires.

Energy slumps are also an invitation for you to peek at your overall diet and make sure it's well-rounded and nutrient-packed. Juices and smoothies are your first step toward maximizing your intake of phytonutrients. But a well-rounded diet that incorporates lots of quality foods—greens, veggies, nuts, seeds, whole grains, legumes, healthy fats, and protein—is also an essential way of ensuring your own vitality and strength.

## How do I get my partner or kids to try green drinks?

One of the nicest things about smoothies and juices is that the recipes are easy to modify in ways that will be immediately palatable to skeptical newbies, old and young. Start with some super tasty blends, and you'll get them on the leafy green bandwagon, too. For juices, I recommend Sweet Greens (page 138) or Green Me Up (page 130). My Easygoing Green (page 199) and Island Green (page 201) are perfect starter smoothies.

Smoothies and juices can also be treated as go-to indulgences for you and yours. Get your kids into the habit of sipping on fiber-rich, antioxidant-packed smoothies in place of conventional (read: crummy) treats. My Creamsicle smoothie (page 241) has all of the flavors of the creamy classic frozen dessert, without any of the refined sugars (and it's got a whole lot of vitamin C and healthy fat, to boot). The Mood Lift (page 268) and the Mint Chip Champion (page 229) are perfect alternatives to chocolate milk. If your kids love orange juice, try sneaking in more fruits and veggies by treating them to a diluted Citrus Shine (page 189) or Crimson Dawn (page 155) juice instead.

## My kids love the way green smoothies taste, but they just can't get over the green color. What can I do?

Hey, you're not the only one. A lot of grown-ups struggle with the color of green drinks, too. Best solution: use plenty of berries in your smoothies. Not only will they mask the hue, they're also packed with antioxidants. Raw cacao powder will also help. Here's a sneaky trick for kids: pour their smoothie in a colored glass or sippy cup. Poof, no greens here! Another idea is to make it fun. Include your kids in the prep and even let them name the recipes. The "green monster" they participated in creating will probably be more interesting to guzzle than a concoction that's forced upon them.

**PART TWO**

# lip-smackin' recipes

# JOYFUL
# JUICES

# THE CLEANSERS

Green is the theme of this whole collection, and these ten juices put it front and center. These are my alkalizing superheroes, the juices you'll want to make again and again to ensure that you're maximizing energy and well-being. Tired? Cranky? Feel a cold coming on? Craving pizza? Allow these green formulas to help you energize and reboot.

# mellow green

A perfect juice for when you're craving something green, but not too green. Pears and cucumber are a heavenly duo, and Swiss chard adds some extra alkaline power to the recipe. Keep in mind that Swiss chard leaves can vary dramatically in size; if your leaves are giant (as big as two hands), one single leaf might be enough for the recipe. To vary the flavor, try adding a few sprigs of mint. Voilà!

Makes 2 Servings (16 to 20 Ounces)

**2 Bartlett or Bosc pears, cored and seeded**

**1 cucumber**

**2 leaves Swiss chard**

1   Wash and prep all ingredients.

2   Juice all ingredients.

# classic green lemonade

Green lemonade is the Cadillac of juicing recipes. This is my take on the beloved classic. The juice is a little sweet (thanks to the apple) and a little spicy (gracias to the ginger). The natural bitterness of leafy greens is cut by a bright squeeze of lemon. You can use almost any type of leafy green in place of chard or kale. Romaine, baby spinach, collard, bok choy, broccoli—you name it! In fact, I love adding broccoli stems to this recipe. Get creative. This juice is a perfect vehicle for all of your greenest fridge scraps.

### Makes 2 Servings (16 to 20 Ounces)

**2 stalks celery**

**1 small cucumber**

**1 apple, cored and seeded**

**1-inch piece ginger, peeled**

**3 leaves Swiss chard or kale**

**½ lemon, peeled**

1   Wash and prep all ingredients.

2   Juice all ingredients.

# soothing green

The name says it all: this is a simple, soothing, and refreshing blend, perfect for showing off the beautiful sweetness of ripe summer honeydew. Feel free to adjust the mint to suit your tastes (I like it nice and minty), and to use any variety of leafy green.

Makes 2 Servings (16 to 20 Ounces)

**4 leaves Swiss chard**

**1 cucumber**

**3 to 4 tablespoons mint leaves, tightly packed, to taste**

**3 cups honeydew melon cubes**

1 Wash and prep all ingredients.
2 Juice all ingredients.

# green me up

This recipe is purrrfect for newbies. It packs a ton of alkaline greens and sweetens them up with a kick of pineapple and pear. The enzymes in bromelain, one of the main compounds in pineapple, have been associated with anti-inflammatory effects, and can aid in digestion, too. Delicious and powerful!

Makes 2 Servings (16 to 20 Ounces)

**2 small stalks celery**

**1 cup pineapple cubes**

**1 Bosc pear, cored and seeded**

**2 leaves Swiss chard**

**2 leaves kale**

**¼ cup parsley, leaves and stems, tightly packed**

**1 cucumber**

1   Wash and prep all ingredients.

2   Juice all ingredients.

# cooling greens

This refresher is made from equal parts love, green juice, and fresh young coconut water, and it's a wonderfully alkaline and hydrating treat. If you're avoiding higher-sugar fruits, mixing coconut water into green drinks is a nice way to add subtle sweetness.

### COCONUT WATER

Coconut water is widely available these days. I like the raw, unpasteurized stuff, which is richer in enzymes and a whole lot tastier than pasteurized varieties. My favorite brands are Harmless Harvest, Exotic Superfoods, and Copra. Most of them can be found at health-food stores or ordered online; you may even be able to find them at your local grocery store.

Alternately, you can open a young Thai coconut at home and reserve the meat for another recipe. (See my tips for opening a young coconut on page 77.)

Makes 2 Servings (16 to 20 Ounces)

**1 small cucumber**

**5 leaves romaine lettuce**

**2 leaves kale**

**2 stalks celery**

**¼ lime, peeled**

**1 cup coconut water**

1  Wash and prep all ingredients.

2  Juice all ingredients except for coconut water.

3  Add coconut water to the juice mixture. Stir and serve.

THE CLEANSERS

# sweet & sour green

A delicious combination of eye-opening orange and pine-apple, mixed with hydrating, alkaline veggies. To make this drink even greener (AKA more powerful), try increasing the spinach or throwing in a fistful of cleansing parsley.

Makes 2 Servings (16 to 20 Ounces)

1 small cucumber

3 stalks celery

1 cup spinach, tightly packed

1 cup pineapple cubes

1 navel orange, peeled

1 Wash and prep all ingredients.

2 Juice all ingredients.

# heavy hitter

If you're hardcore, friends, then this is your juice. It's a fruit-free, super green blend that's ideal for those who are seeking heavy alkalinity and plenty of cleansing power. It's also an ideal option for those of you who are looking to cut back on sugar.

This juice demonstrates how effectively ginger and lemon work to offset the natural bitterness of greens. But if the mixture is too intense for you, throw in a small apple or pear for a little sweetness.

Makes 2 Servings (16 to 20 Ounces)

**2 leaves kale**
**5 leaves dandelion greens**
**1 large cucumber**
**4 stalks celery**
**1-inch piece ginger, peeled**
**½ lemon, peeled**

1   Wash and prep all ingredients.
2   Juice all ingredients.

# green & sassy

Granny Smith apples are lower in sugar than other varieties, and contain a tart and tasty kick. Plus the ginger and
lemon make this blend especially energizing. Feel free to
add more lemon and ginger for some extra sass.

Makes 2 Servings (16 to 20 Ounces)

**2 Granny Smith apples, cored and seeded**

**1 cucumber**

**2 stalks celery**

**½ lemon, peeled**

**1-inch piece ginger**

**¼ cup parsley, leaves and stems, tightly packed**

1   Wash and prep all ingredients.

2   Juice all ingredients.

# spicy sweetie

This juice recipe is the perfect marriage of zesty and slightly sweet, and it's one of my favorite elixirs. Like most of its fellow green leafy vegetables, arugula is high in vitamin K, which supports bone health. It's also rich in glucosinolates, sulfur-containing compounds that can help release the vegetable's phytochemicals. Arugula is also a lovely addition to green juices because it's got a slightly spicy flavor, especially when it's purchased at the height of freshness. Baby arugula, which is carried in grocery stores year-round, is more mellow.

**PRO TIP** If this juice isn't quite sweet enough for you, you can try using two pears in place of the tart Granny Smith apples.

Makes 2 Servings (16 to 20 Ounces)

**2 cups green cabbage, tightly packed**

**2 cups arugula, leaves and stems, tightly packed**

**1 small cucumber**

**2 large stalks celery**

**2 Granny Smith apples**

**1-inch piece ginger, peeled**

1   Wash and prep all ingredients.

2   Juice all ingredients.

THE CLEANSERS

137

# sweet greens

Fresh watermelon creates an irresistible sweetness that will win over even the stubbornest green juice skeptics. Just keep in mind that juices made with watermelon taste best when the fruit is used in season—underripe, spongy, or dry melons taste a little bitter. You can freeze fresh melon cubes for a few months.

**Makes 2 Servings (16 to 20 Ounces)**

**2½ cups watermelon cubes**

**2 cups spinach, packed**

**1 cucumber**

**¼ lime**

1   Wash and prep all ingredients.

2   Juice all ingredients.

# THE HEALERS

Plant foods are healing across the board, but the following juices are designed to have a particularly medicinal effect on the body. Whether you're hoping to boost your immunity, soothe your digestion, fight inflammation, or give yourself a dose of protection against chronic disease or hypertension, you're sure to find a suitable elixir here.

# root power

This recipe is all about root vegetables: beets, carrots, and daikon radish. Though not a common juice ingredient, daikon is a healthy-spicy addition to any blend. The long, pale white-colored root vegetable is often used in traditional Chinese medicine to help aid digestion and enhance immunity. It's also a mild diuretic, which makes this a handy juice formula when you're feeling a little bloated.

### Makes 2 Servings (16 to 20 Ounces)

**1 small beet**

**2 Granny Smith apples, cored and seeded**

**4 medium carrots**

**½ small daikon radish (about 5 inches)**

**1 cucumber**

**1-inch piece ginger, peeled**

1 Wash and prep all ingredients.

2 Juice all ingredients.

# garden-in-a-glass

The name says it all. This juice is a vegetable all-star, brimming with powerful phytonutrients. It's mildly sweet (and delish!) thanks to the beet and carrots. But feel free to mix it up a bit. This recipe is a great opportunity to use up those vegetable odds and ends. Cucumber half? Throw it in. Some leftover leaves of lettuce or romaine? Add 'em in. Be playful, and enjoy every nutrient-dense sip.

### Makes 2 Servings (16 to 20 Ounces)

**2 medium carrots**

**1 small beet**

**2 stalks celery**

**1 cucumber**

**¼ cup parsley, leaves and stems, tightly packed**

**1 small broccoli stem**

**4 leaves romaine**

**½ lemon, peeled**

**1-inch piece ginger, peeled**

1   Wash and prep all ingredients.

2   Juice all ingredients.

# 16 ounces of prevention

Back off disease, there's a new sheriff in town—this righ-teous juice! It's an anti-inflammatory, immune-boosting powerhouse. Betalain, an antioxidant in beets, can tame the flames and support the detoxification process, while ginger has both antiviral and antibacterial properties. Pears and romaine lettuce help to make this juice as sweet and refreshing as it is healthy.

### Makes 2 Servings (16 to 20 Ounces)

**1 small beet**
**2 pears, cored and seeded**
**½ head romaine lettuce (about 8 to 10 leaves)**
**1 cup spinach, tightly packed**
**1-inch piece ginger, peeled**

1   Wash and prep all ingredients.
2   Juice all ingredients.

# immune boost

If your immune system is in SOS mode, then this is the juice for you. Oranges provide loads of vitamin C, which may aid in immune system deficiencies, and carrots have been shown to have a protective effect against multiple cancers (in addition to their famous vision-boosting superpowers!). Turmeric root is a potent anti-inflammatory agent, and if you're starting to get the sniffles, the dash of cayenne will help you sweat them out ASAP. Use one shake if you're sensitive to spice, two to three if you like it red hot.

### Makes 2 Servings (16 to 20 Ounces)

**4 large carrots**
**2 navel oranges, peeled**
**½-inch piece turmeric root**
**Pinch of cayenne pepper**

1   Wash and prep all ingredients.
2   Juice all ingredients.

# reboot ready

We tend to overlook watercress among the leafy greens, but we shouldn't: this crucifer is known for protecting skin against aging damage, and it's packed with vitamins A, K, and C, which means healthy bones and hair to boot!

Watercress has a very distinctive, somewhat spicy flavor, so it's best to use it in moderation, I like a combination of watercress and a more mellow green such as baby spinach, but you can use romaine, too.

Makes 2 Servings (16 to 20 Ounces)

½ cup watercress, leaves and stems, tightly packed
½ cup baby spinach, tightly packed
1 cucumber
2 stalks celery
1 large pear, cored and seeded
¼ lime, peeled

1   Wash and prep all ingredients.
2   Juice all ingredients.

# simple greens & carrot

What's up, doc? Bugs would be pleased with this simple blend of carrots and greens. This juice is moderately sweet and full of alkaline greens, not to mention a healthy dose of beta-carotene from the carrots. If you're not a carrot lover, you can replace them with two Granny Smith apples or one to two small beets.

### Makes 2 Servings (16 to 20 Ounces)

**3 medium carrots**

**1 cucumber**

**1 large stalk celery**

**¼ cup parsley, leaves and stems, tightly packed**

**½ head romaine lettuce, leaves only (about 8 to 10 leaves)**

1   Wash and prep all ingredients.

2   Juice all ingredients.

THE HEALERS

# c bomb

This immunity-boosting beverage is all about vitamin C, which may also help to prevent high blood pressure and high cholesterol. Win-win! I love the purple-haze color that red cabbage lends to this sweet-spicy juice, but green cabbage is a fine replacement if you don't have red on hand.

Makes 2 Servings (16 to 20 Ounces)

1 cucumber

4 stalks celery

2 small apples, cored and seeded

1½ cups red cabbage

1-inch piece of ginger, peeled

1   Wash and prep all ingredients.

2   Juice all ingredients.

# ginger aid

This simple and fuss-free blend shows off the signature flavor and healing properties of ginger root. Ginger has long been celebrated for its antinausea properties, so make this your go-to tonic for occasional indigestion. While you sip, you can rest assured that ginger root is also helping to cool inflammation and fight the aging process.

**PRO TIP** To give this juice even more alkaline power, try throwing in an extra fistful of spinach (or a few leaves of romaine).

### Makes 2 Servings (16 to 20 Ounces)

**1½ cups spinach**

**1 large cucumber**

**2 stalks celery**

**1 large pear, cored and seeded**

**1-inch piece ginger, peeled**

1   Wash and prep all ingredients.

2   Juice all ingredients.

# belly soother

A gentle blend for irritated digestive tracts. Aloe juice is thought to help soothe ulcerations (it relieves constipation, too), while mint is thought to improve bile flow into the stomach, which can help to speed digestion and ease indigestion.

In addition to the aloe, this juice features other calming ingredients. Cucumber, honeydew, and pear are all inflammation fighters, and cucumber is also a good source of magnesium, which can help to tame stress.

### Makes 2 Servings (16 to 20 Ounces)

1 large cucumber

1½ cups honeydew melon cubes

1 pear, cored and seeded

5 stalks romaine

⅛ cup mint leaves, tightly packed

1 to 2 teaspoons aloe juice

1   Wash and prep all ingredients.

2   Juice all ingredients except for the aloe juice.

3   Stir aloe juice into the finished juice.

## ALOE VERA

Bottled aloe vera juice can be easily added to juices or smoothies. It's a great ingredient to keep handy if you're prone to irritable digestion—especially constipation. The taste of aloe is quite distinctive, so start by adding ½ teaspoon at a time and increasing as desired.

You should be able to find aloe vera juice at any health-food store; just ask a salesperson where it's located. I like the Lily of the Desert and Fruit of the Earth brands. Nature's Way also makes a good aloe vera juice. All three of these brands can also be found online.

# crimson dawn

Good morning, gorgeous! It's time to strut your stuff. This juice is a perfect wakeup call. I love the combination of zippy citrus and grounding root vegetables. You'll also get a hit of red bell pepper, which is an incredible source of vitamin C. Forget those cold-fighting powders and lozenges, and try a sip of this immune-boosting elixir instead. Now go kick some butt!

Makes 2 Servings (16 to 20 Ounces)

**4 medium carrots**

**1 medium beet**

**1 large navel orange, peeled**

**1 red bell pepper, stem and seeds removed**

**2 stalks celery**

**¾–1 inch piece ginger, peeled**

1   Wash and prep all ingredients.

2   Juice all ingredients.

# tummy tamer

Fennel has long been known as a balm for all sorts of digestive woes, from indigestion and heartburn to bloating and irregularity. It's thought to stimulate bile secretion, which can help keep digestion running smoothly and allow you to assimilate your food efficiently.

In this refreshing and mildly sweet juice, fennel meets ginger—another belly-soothing superstar—and hydrating cucumber. The combination of ingredients can help to keep nausea and bloating at bay. This is a perfect elixir to sip before or after a heavy meal.

### Makes 2 Servings (16 to 20 Ounces)

½ small head fennel (about ½ cup)
1 large or 2 small cucumbers
2 stalks celery
⅛ cup mint, leaves and stems, tightly packed
2 apples
1-inch piece ginger, peeled

1   Wash and prep all ingredients.
2   Juice all ingredients.

**THE HEALERS**

# the sicilian

This vegetable-packed elixir first appeared in *Crazy Sexy Kitchen*, and it won us over with its spicy and satisfying taste. It's hearty and savory, just the recipe you'll want when your tummy's rumbling. The celery in this juice provides phthalide, a phytochemical that can help to relax the smooth muscles of the arteries and lower blood pressure. The garlic provides not only a zesty taste, but also plenty of immunity-boosting antibacterial properties. As the Italians would say, "Bevi!"

**PRO TIP** Be sure to remove all seeds from the jalapeño pepper before running it through your juicer. Most of the zing is housed in the seeds, and they can overpower your juice if they happen to slip in!

### Makes 2 Servings (16 to 20 Ounces)

**6 medium carrots**

**3 large tomatoes**

**2 red bell peppers**

**2 cloves garlic**

**4 stalks celery**

**1 cup watercress**

**1 cup loosely packed spinach**

**1 red jalapeño, seeded (optional)**

1   Wash and prep all ingredients.

2   Juice all ingredients.

# THE BOOSTERS

These juices are on the sweeter side, which means that they're perfect for a healthy energy boost. Struggling with the 3 P.M. lull? Hoping to make a fruity and refreshing summer drink for a get-together with friends? Allow these juices to lift your spirits. The boosters are also a great option for those of us who are a little skittish about the taste of greens.

If you love these energizing recipes, but you're being mindful of the sweetness in your juices, simply follow my tips on page 53 for reducing the sugar content of juices or smoothies.

# orange uplift

This sunny, sweet, refreshing juice is a wonderful morning wake-up call. There's no actual orange in here, but cantaloupe and carrots help to create a vibrant color. Cantaloupe is a superstar source of vitamins A and C, both of which help to keep your skin and eyes healthy and your immune system strong. Cantaloupe is also rich in potassium, which aids in hydration and helps to keep your blood pressure steady.

**PRO TIP** To make this mixture slightly less sweet, try substituting one cucumber for the carrots.

### Makes 2 Servings (16 to 20 Ounces)

**2 cups cantaloupe cubes**

**2 medium carrots**

**4 stalks celery**

**½ head romaine lettuce (about 8 to 10 leaves)**

1   Wash and prep all ingredients.

2   Juice all ingredients.

# blueberry lemon-aid

Conventional lemonade recipes are packed with added sugars (and the bottled ones have some not-so-savory additives and preservatives, too). This mixture evokes the beloved taste of freshly made lemonade, but it's infused with body-boosting ingredients. The cucumbers create a hydrating base for the juice, while apples provide a lovely sweetness that's not too sugary. The fresh blueberries add age-defying antioxidants and help give the drink a gorgeous purple color.

**PRO TIP** This is another great recipe to keep handy for summer entertaining, or to offer kids as a more nutritious spin on a favorite childhood classic!

Makes 2 Servings (16 to 20 Ounces)

**2 small cucumbers**

**1 cup blueberries**

**2 Granny Smith apples**

**¼ lemon, peeled**

**3 tablespoons mint leaves, tightly packed**

1  Wash and prep all ingredients.

2  Juice all ingredients.

# tangy trip

You may be used to roasting fennel or shaving it into salads, but prepare to be amazed at the very subtle sweetness it lends to juices, as well as a mellow hint of licorice flavor. Along with its properties as a digestive aid (see my Tummy Tamer recipe on page 157), fennel can give your skin a boost. It contains quercetin, a phytochemical that may help to protect against harmful UV ray damage, as well as other anti-inflammatory flavonoids.

**Makes 2 Servings (16 to 20 Ounces)**

**½ small head fennel (about ½ cup)**

**1 cucumber**

**2 stalks celery**

**1½ cups pineapple cubes**

**4 leaves romaine**

**¼ lemon, peeled**

1  Wash and prep all ingredients.

2  Juice all ingredients.

# green & gold

This juice is light and refreshing—a spectacular combo for hot summer afternoons. If you don't have apples, you can substitute pears (or fresh melon). If you're easing your way into the wonderful world of green juices, try substituting romaine leaves for the kale in equal proportions—they'll have a slightly milder taste.

Makes 2 Servings (16 to 20 Ounces)

**2 cups pineapple cubes**
**2 small apples, cored and seeded**
**1-inch piece ginger, peeled**
**6 leaves kale**
**¼ cup mint leaves, tightly packed**

1   Wash and prep all ingredients.
2   Juice all ingredients.

# pretty in pink

This electric pink juice is a beet lover's dream! The combination of pineapple and Granny Smith apple is as delightfully tart as it is sweet. Plus, ginger adds a little heat to the mixture. To lessen the sweetness of the juice, try substituting a cucumber for the apple and adding a handful of mild greens, like spinach or romaine.

### Makes 2 Servings (16 to 20 Ounces)

**2 cups pineapple, cubed**
**1 Granny Smith apple, cored and seeded**
**1 medium beet**
**1-inch piece ginger, peeled**

1   Wash and prep all ingredients.
2   Juice all ingredients.

# herbal elixer

This cheery drink is an ode to summer's most beloved ingredients, from cucumber to pineapple to fresh basil. I recommend making it seasonally, when your herbs and fruits are at the peak of freshness. Basil contains tons of flavonoids that can help to protect your skin against aging and UV damage.

Makes 2 Servings (16 to 20 Ounces)

**1 large cucumber**
**2½ cups pineapple cubes**
**¼ cup basil, leaves and stems, tightly packed**
**¼ cup cilantro or parsley, leaves and stems, tightly packed**
**⅛ cup mint leaves, tightly packed**
**4 stalks kale**

1   Wash and prep all ingredients.
2   Juice all ingredients.

# blushing beauty

Peaches and yum! This juice is both herbal and fruity, a light and unusual combination. You'll be delighted at the taste (and dusty rose color) that strawberries and peaches lend to the elixir. You can also feel good about the fact that this juice is like a liquid prescription for beautiful skin! It's incredibly high in vitamin C, which helps us to form collagen (an important structural component of strong skin) and fight off free radicals. Peaches are also high in beta-carotene, which is associated with cell repair.

**PRO TIP** You can substitute other summer berries, like blackberries or raspberries, for the strawberries in this recipe.

### Makes 2 Servings (16 to 20 Ounces)

**1 large cucumber**

**2 large peaches, pitted**

**3 cups strawberries**

**2 tablespoons basil leaves, tightly packed**

1   Wash and prep all ingredients.

2   Juice all ingredients.

# tropical tease

Dance on a table by the beach with this sultry—yet refreshing—cocktail of alkaline greens and zesty pineapple. If you love spice, feel free to add more jalapeños to the mix—but be prepared for a kick! If you're sensitive to heat, start with half of an average-size jalapeño pepper and take it from there.

Makes 2 Servings (16 to 20 Ounces)

2 small cucumbers

2 cups pineapple cubes

⅓ cup cilantro, leaves and stems, tightly packed

1 cup spinach, tightly packed

½ to 1 small jalapeño, seeds removed

1   Wash and prep all ingredients.

2   Juice all ingredients.

# rise 'n' shine

Up and at 'em with this sweet and tart breakfast juice.
Carrots, pineapple, and grapefruit make a potently energizing trio, and ginger gives the recipe a little zip. For an
even more eye-opening, zippy experience, try adding a
whole inch of ginger to the mix. Hello, Dolly!

Makes 2 Servings (16 to 20 Ounces)

**5 medium carrots**
**1 pink grapefruit, peeled**
**2 cups pineapple cubes**
**½-inch piece ginger, peeled**

1  Wash and prep all ingredients.
2  Juice all ingredients.

# feelin' hot, hot, hot

Spice up your juice routine with this unusual blend of mellow honeydew and spicy jalapeño. I love to drink this one as a cocktail on hot summer nights; the cilantro is a wonderfully refreshing addition. As always, adjust the jalapeño to suit your taste (and tolerance for heat!).

**PRO TIP** If you don't have ripe honeydew on hand, try watermelon instead.

### Makes 2 Servings (16 to 20 Ounces)

1½ cups honeydew melon cubes

2 leaves kale

¼ cup cilantro, leaves and stems, tightly packed

1 large cucumber

1 to 2 jalapeño peppers, seeds removed

1   Wash and prep all ingredients.

2   Juice all ingredients.

# pucker up

This sassy breakfast blend is a fire hose of sunshine—and it's anti-inflammatory, antibacterial, and immune boosting to boot! Citrus and ginger are a delightful combination, and I love the balance of tart grapefruit and sweet oranges. Lemon gives the juice an extra dose of pucker (and an alkaline boost, too).

Makes 2 Servings (16 to 20 Ounces)

1 pink grapefruit, peeled
3 navel oranges, peeled
½-inch piece turmeric root
1-inch piece ginger, peeled
¼ lemon, peeled

1 Wash and prep all ingredients.
2 Juice all ingredients.

# THE BEAUTIFIERS

One of the most wonderful features of fruits and vegetables is that we can reap their benefits inside and out. The next ten juices are full of ingredients that can help to make our skin brighter and more radiant, antioxidants that will help to slow down the aging process, and ingredients that can bust bloat and keep us hydrated.

# aloe force

This drink leads a double life as a digestive remedy and a skin soother. In addition to its belly soothing properties, aloe is said to speed the healing of mouth ulcers and combat skin conditions like psoriasis and dermatitis. Other beneficial and skin soothing ingredients in this mellow cocktail are hydrating cucumber and anti-inflammatory ginger.

Makes 2 Servings (16 to 20 Ounces)

2 medium carrots

1 large cucumber

2 large stalks celery

1 apple, cored and seeded

¼ lemon, peeled

1 teaspoon aloe juice

½-inch piece ginger, peeled

1   Wash and prep all ingredients.

2   Juice all ingredients except for the aloe juice.

3   Stir aloe juice into the finished juice.

# skin sweetie

We don't always think of berries as juicing staples (most of us are more accustomed to throwing them into smoothies), but this tart and tasty blend proves that berries can add tons of flavor and subtle sweetness to our juice tonics. This juice features two fruits with potent antiaging properties: blueberries (antioxidant superstars) and kiwis (which are packed with vitamin C, an ally in collagen formation and free radical defense). The result is an elixir that will keep your complexion dewy and youthful while also tickling your taste buds.

### Makes 2 Servings (16 to 20 Ounces)

**1 cup spinach, tightly packed**

**5 leaves romaine**

**1 large cucumber**

**1½ cups blueberries**

**3 kiwis, peeled**

1   Wash and prep all ingredients.

2   Juice all ingredients.

# brighten & lighten

I love the fresh tartness of this juice, which is a little sweet and a lot tangy. I also love that it features Swiss chard, which is packed with many of the same nutrients (vitamins A, K, and C) as other leafy greens, but is also rich in B vitamins, to help keep your energy levels high (and your skin sparkly). The enzymes in chard are also associated with blood sugar regulation, which makes this a great cocktail to boost your mood while keeping your hunger and energy stable.

### Makes 2 Servings (16 to 20 Ounces)

**1 large Granny Smith apple**

**1 cup spinach, leaves and stems, tightly packed**

**1 cucumber**

**2 leaves Swiss chard**

**2 stalks celery**

**¼ cup cilantro, leaves and stems, tightly packed**

**¼ lemon, peeled**

1  Wash and prep all ingredients.

2  Juice all ingredients.

# go go glow!

Clean, smooth, and simple, this juice is ideal for an everyday, alkaline treat. It's also a perfect skin tonic. Dandelion is thought to be soothing for the skin, and it's also a diuretic, which will help to keep your complexion taut and toned. The potassium in dandelion greens, combined with the hydrating properties of cucumber, will also help to give your cheeks the "glow."

Though dandelion can taste slightly bitter, this recipe perfectly balances the bitterness with the mellow sweetness of pear and the tartness of lemon.

### Makes 2 Servings (16 to 20 Ounces)

**1 large pear, cored and seeded**

**1 large cucumber**

**2 leaves Swiss chard**

**8 leaves dandelion greens**

**¼ lemon, peeled**

1   Wash and prep all ingredients.

2   Juice all ingredients.

# cleansing kick

This recipe was inspired by the famous lemon, maple syrup, and cayenne drink that's often known as the "master cleanse." While this has a similar flavor, its primary nutritional benefit is the anti-inflammatory power from ginger and turmeric. These spices add additional heat and a brilliant orange color to the cocktail.

**PRO TIP** Since it's a lot of work to juice the first three ingredients, I like to make double or even triple batches of the lemon, ginger, and turmeric juice at once, mixing them with the other ingredients over the course of a few days. If you have a twin gear or masticating juicer, you'll be able to prepare enough for seconds—or thirds! The juice will last for up to three days in an airtight container in the fridge, or up to one month in the freezer.

Makes 2 Servings (16 to 20 Ounces)

**1 lemon, peeled**

**1-inch piece ginger, peeled**

**1-inch piece turmeric, peeled**

**2 tablespoons maple syrup**

**Pinch of cayenne pepper**

1   Wash and prep all ingredients

2   Juice the lemon, ginger, and turmeric.

3   Whisk 2 cups water with the maple syrup and cayenne into the juice mixture.

THE BEAUTIFIERS

# bloat buster

Belly bloat got you down? Then it's time for a sip of this refreshing, clean juice. It's a honeydew lover's delight, featuring a mixture of fresh melon and a gaggle of greens. The parsley and dandelion greens act as a gentle and natural diuretic, helping you to shed water weight and feel less puffy. Make this your cocktail of choice when PMS calls, when you've been too busy to hydrate properly, or when you simply need to feel refreshed.

### Makes 2 Servings (16 to 20 Ounces)

**6 leaves dandelion greens**

**1 large cucumber**

**2 large leaves Swiss chard**

**⅛ cup parsley, leaves and stems, tightly packed**

**2 cups honeydew melon cubes**

1 Wash and prep all ingredients.

2 Juice all ingredients.

# citrus shine

Pucker, power, pow! This delightful formula will help kick-start your day with a medley of sweet and sour flavors. Tart apple, orange, and lemon are mellowed out by sweet kiwi and the hydrating cucumber.

Makes 2 Servings (16 to 20 Ounces)

**1 kiwi**

**1 medium apple, cored and seeded**

**1 navel orange, peeled**

**2 cucumbers**

**½ lemon**

1 Wash and prep all ingredients.

2 Juice all ingredients.

# hello hydration

I absolutely adore this combination of three simple ingredients—it's like a summery Italian salad in a glass! Watermelon lends irresistible sweetness to the mixture, while the cucumber and the savory addition of basil mellow it out. You'll want to make this juice when watermelon is ripe—so it's worth waiting until summer. Serve it to friends at cookouts, garden parties, or brunches, and be prepared to smile at their ooh's and ah's.

Makes 2 Servings (16 to 20 Ounces)

**1 large cucumber**

**3 cups watermelon**

**¼ cup basil, leaves and stems, tightly packed**

1   Wash and prep all ingredients.

2   Juice all ingredients.

# fatigue fighter

This vivacious juice will pick you up and get you going with a touch of sweetness from pears and grapes and hints of tartness from the lime. Pears are rich in vitamin B2, which plays a crucial role in energy production and helps us metabolize iron—an important nutrient in maintaining energy levels. Some studies suggest that grapes may help to boost cognitive function (always useful!). Make this your go-to juice cocktail for those mornings when you need a little extra brain and body power.

### Makes 2 Servings (16 to 20 Ounces)

**8 leaves romaine**

**1 cup spinach, tightly packed**

**2 stalks celery**

**1 pear**

**1½ cups grapes, green or red**

**¼ lime, peeled**

1  Wash and prep all ingredients.

2  Juice all ingredients.

# 8

# SCRUMPTIOUS SMOOTHIES

# THE pH WARRIORS: GREEN SMOOTHIES

Like the "cleansers" in my juice section, these recipes feature greens prominently. They are the smoothies I return to again and again, the recipes I keep handy for breakfast or a meal on-the-go. These alkalizing blends will help anyone to fall in love with fresh greens—including wonderful you!

# green power protein

Make this your go-to smoothie when you need to feel ready to take on the world. Hemp seeds don't need to be soaked, which means that you can throw a few tablespoons into your smoothie and blend away.

## MACA

Indigenous to South America, maca has been used traditionally for centuries to help balance hormones (and boost libido—*meow*). It's also a great energy enhancer. Maca has a distinctive, earthy flavor, so I recommend starting with a small quantity and increasing your intake gradually.

Chances are, you can find maca in your local health-food store. It's also widely available online. I love the Navitas Naturals and Sunfoods brands.

Makes 2 Servings (16 to 20 Ounces)

**1 banana, frozen**

**½ apple, cored and seeded**

**1½ cups cashew hemp milk (page 276) or nondairy milk of choice**

**2 tablespoons shelled hemp seeds**

**1 teaspoon maca powder**

**1 pitted Medjool date**

**2 cups spinach, tightly packed**

1    Wash and prep all ingredients.

2    Blend and serve.

# easygoing green

The name says it all. This green smoothie is easy to love.
It's also super hydrating, thanks to the addition of coconut
water, and chock-full of healthy fats from the avocado.
The more avocado you add, the thicker the texture will be,
so feel free to add up to half a Hass avocado if you'd like
something a little thicker (see my tips for storing leftover
avocado halves on page 74).

Makes 2 Servings (16 to 20 Ounces)

1 large banana, frozen

1 cup mango cubes, frozen

2 cups coconut water (see page 131 for my favorite brands)

¼ Hass avocado

¼ cup curly parsley, stems and leaves, tightly packed

1 cup kale, leaves only, tightly packed

1   Wash and prep all ingredients.

2   Blend and serve.

# deep blue green

I want to swim in the ocean of this gorgeously colored recipe. Aside from its purdy hue, blue and purple fruits and vegetables are associated with anthocyanins, antioxidants that may help to prevent heart disease by lowering inflammation. The ground flax in this smoothie also provides a heart-healthy and anti-inflammatory dose of omega-3 fatty acids.

Makes 2 Servings (16 to 20 Ounces)

**1 cup seedless grapes (green or red)**
**¾ cup blueberries, frozen**
**1½ cups coconut water**
**1 tablespoon flax seeds, ground**
**1 cup kale, leaves only, tightly packed**
**¼ Hass avocado**

1   Wash and prep all ingredients.
2   Blend and serve.

# island green

Get your sarong, we're going to the Bahamas with this lovely blend of tropical fruit, greens, and nourishing coconut. Spirulina, an algae that is thought to aid immunity and memory, is another fabulous feature of this smoothie, and it helps to give it a gorgeous, blue-green hue. If the idea of hacking open a coconut at home scares you, don't worry: my tutorial on page 77 will tell you everything you need to know (and give you a store-bought coconut option, too).

### Makes 2 Servings (16 to 20 Ounces)

1 banana, frozen

1 cup pineapple cubes

½ cup young Thai coconut meat

1½ cups coconut water

1 cup kale, tightly packed

¼ cup cilantro, leaves and stems, tightly packed

½ teaspoon spirulina

1   Wash and prep all ingredients.

2   Blend and serve.

# calming greens

This smoothie is a go-to in our home. I love the refreshing addition of cilantro and mint, and avocado creates a luscious texture. If you don't happen to have grapes handy, try kiwi or honeydew melon in their place. If you do have grapes, oh boy, you're gonna be happy.

### Makes 2 Servings (16 to 20 Ounces)

**1 banana, frozen**

**1 cup green grapes**

**¼ Hass avocado**

**⅓ cup cilantro, leaves and stems, tightly packed**

**¼ cup fresh mint leaves, tightly packed**

**1 cup spinach, tightly packed**

**1¼ cups water**

1   Wash and prep all ingredients.

2   In a high-speed blender, blend all ingredients. Serve.

# peachy green

This recipe was inspired by my favorite summer fruit stand—the peaches are out-of-control delicious and juicy. I buy one for my bike ride home and the rest for smoothies! In this blend, peaches and banana meet heart-healthy flax seeds and a creamy base of cashew hemp milk.

### Makes 2 Servings (16 to 20 Ounces)

**1 large banana, frozen**

**1 cup peaches, peeled, pitted, and cut into chunks or slices (fresh or frozen)**

**1 tablespoon flax seeds, ground**

**1½ cups cashew hemp milk (page 276) or nondairy milk of choice**

**1 cup Swiss chard, washed, stems removed, and torn into pieces (about 2 large leaves), tightly packed**

1   Wash and prep all ingredients.

2   Blend and serve.

# savory green

We often think of smoothies as being fruity, but they don't have to be. In fact, different combinations of greens, avocado, salt, and lemon are one of my staple blends—especially when I'm hoping to get a lot of alkaline goodness without any added sugar.

**PRO TIP** Think of this recipe as a template for savory smoothies, and feel free to adjust it based on your tastes. You may want to throw in different combinations of fresh herbs, or alternate a variety of greens instead of spinach. Add a little less avocado for a lighter blend, or a little extra for something very rich and creamy.

Makes 2 Servings (16 to 20 Ounces)

**1 cup baby spinach, tightly packed**

**1 cucumber, peeled and chopped**

**1 tablespoon lemon juice**

**½ Hass avocado**

**¼ teaspoon salt**

**½ to 1 teaspoon garlic, minced (optional)**

**1 teaspoon olive oil or flax oil**

**2 tablespoons fresh parsley, basil, or tarragon, packed (optional)**

**¾ cup water**

1   Wash and prep all ingredients.

2   In a high-speed blender, blend all ingredients till totally smooth. Serve.

# green bliss

Bliss out with this addictive combination of banana, pear, creamy cashew hemp milk, and greens. Plus, the lemon gives it a subtle zing of freshness. This smoothie is also an opportunity to pack two types of leafy greens into your blender. If you don't happen to have spinach and romaine, try another combination based on what you've got or what looks good at the market.

Makes 2 Servings (16 to 20 Ounces)

**1 banana, frozen**

**1 pear, cored and seeded**

**1½ cups cashew hemp milk (page 276) or nondairy milk of choice**

**1 cup spinach, tightly packed**

**3 large leaves romaine lettuce**

**1 tablespoon freshly squeezed lemon juice**

1  Wash and prep all ingredients.

2  Blend and serve.

THE pH WARRIORS

# detox darling

If detoxing could taste this good all the time, we'd all be fit as fiddles! The sprouts give this blend an earthy, nutty flavor, which is balanced perfectly by sweet pear and banana. Sunflower sprouts are one of the most nutritious sprouts around, featuring plenty of protein, B vitamins, and zinc, the latter of which is essential for immune function, while the leafy greens support your body's natural detoxification processes.

Makes 2 Servings (16 to 20 Ounces)

½ cup dandelion greens, tightly packed

1 cup baby spinach, tightly packed

⅓ cup sunflower sprouts, tightly packed

½ large or 1 small pear, cored and seeded

1 banana, frozen

1½ cups almond milk (page 274) or nondairy milk of choice

1   Wash and prep all ingredients.

2   Blend till smooth and serve.

# granny smith apple pie

Who doesn't love a good ole slice of apple pie? Well, this smoothie is the next best thing. It's sweet, a little tart, and the cinnamon evokes Grandma's favorite dessert perfectly.

## APPLES AND PEARS IN SMOOTHIES

Apples and pears make wonderful additions to smoothies, adding a thick, almost "fluffy" texture to the mix, along with sweetness. If you'd like to add extra fiber to your smoothie, then leave the skin on the fruit. If you'd like your blend to have a smoother texture, then you'll want to peel your apples or pears after you core and seed them.

Makes 2 Servings (20 to 24 Ounces)

**1 banana, frozen**

**1 Granny Smith apple, cored, peeled, and seeded**

**1½ cups kale, leaves only, tightly packed**

**1½ cups pumpkin seed milk (page 288) or nondairy milk of choice**

**¼ teaspoon cinnamon**

**1 pitted Medjool date (optional)**

1   Wash and prep all ingredients.

2   Blend and serve.

# sassy green

Think of this sassy smoothie as alkaline Southern Comfort in a glass. It's bright, it's refreshing, it's a little spicy, but unlike SoCo, it's full of green goodness. Many people think of collard greens as bitter, but they're actually a mild and user-friendly addition to green smoothies—and an intensely healthful one. Collards are full of beta-carotene, which the body converts to vitamin A, an important nutrient for nails, hair, skin, and eyes. They're also rich in cancer-preventing glucosinolates, iron, calcium, and folate. Down the hatch!

Makes 2 Servings (16 to 20 Ounces)

**1 banana, frozen**

**1 navel orange, peeled and quartered**

**½ small cucumber**

**1 cup coconut water**

**½-inch piece ginger, peeled**

**1 cup collard greens, roughly chopped or cut into ribbons, tightly packed**

1   Wash and prep all ingredients.

2   Blend and serve.

# alkaline armor

Who knew that flooding your body with alkaline ingredients could taste so good? This smoothie is packed with alkaline superfoods, including sprouts, cucumber, leafy greens, and avocado. It also features a touch of Granny Smith apple and lemon, which makes it reminiscent of a deliciously creamy, filling green juice. This is a wonderfully healthful way to begin any morning (or to brighten up any afternoon).

Makes 2 Servings (16 to 20 Ounces)

**5 leaves romaine lettuce, roughly chopped**

**⅓ cup sunflower sprouts, tightly packed**

**½ cucumber, peeled**

**¼ Hass avocado**

**1 small Granny Smith apple, cored and seeded**

**1 banana, frozen**

**1 teaspoon lemon juice**

**1½ cups water**

1  Wash and prep all ingredients.

2  Blend till smooth and serve.

THE pH WARRIORS

# THE BODY BOOSTERS

Smoothies are incredibly powerful vehicles for optimum nutrition. The following blends have been designed to help you boost your daily intake of some of the nutrients our bodies' need most dearly: iron, calcium, fatty acids, and protein. If you're being nagged with the "where do you get your protein" question, friends, you can rest assured that these particular recipes are designed to give you a meal-worthy protein boost.

# popeye

Be strong to the finish with this vibrantly colored, delicious green blend. Spinach wins special favor in the vegetable kingdom for its incredible store of anti-inflammatory and cancer-fighting flavonoids, and it's an excellent source of iron. Meanwhile, the mango in this recipe provides 100 percent of your recommended daily dose of superstar antioxidant vitamin C. This smoothie tastes mildly tropical, and it's one of my go-to green blends.

Makes 2 Servings (20 to 24 Ounces)

1 banana, frozen

¼ cup mango cubes, frozen

2 cups spinach, tightly packed

1 teaspoon chia seeds

1⅔ cups pumpkin seed milk (page 288) or nondairy milk of choice

1   Wash and prep all ingredients.

2   Blend and serve.

# sesame superhero

You'll be fighting off foes with this powerful potion. It showcases all of the nutritional superpowers of the humble sesame seed: iron, protein, and calcium. It also contains tons of potassium and vitamins K, A, and C, thanks to banana and a heaping cup of collard greens. Raisins, which are used to sweeten this smoothie in place of the usual Medjool dates, are a great and often overlooked source of iron—plus, they're packed with belly-friendly fiber, too.

### Makes 2 Servings (16 to 20 Ounces)

**1 cup collard greens, cut into ribbons, tightly packed**

**1 large banana, frozen**

**1 tablespoon tahini**

**1½ cups sesame seed milk (page 289) or nondairy milk of choice**

**⅛ cup raisins, packed**

**½ teaspoon vanilla extract or powder**

1   Wash and prep all ingredients.

2   Blend till smooth and serve.

THE BODY BOOSTERS

# body builder

This protein-packed smoothie is my go-to meal before or after a workout. Peanut butter and hemp seeds help to build and repair muscle, while the kale keeps things mean, green, and loaded with minerals like calcium and iron. Substitute any of your favorite nut milks for the almond milk in this recipe; cashew hemp milk (page 276) will give you an added dose of protein, too.

### Makes 2 Servings (20 to 24 Ounces)

2 small bananas, frozen

2 cups almond milk (page 274) or nondairy milk of choice

2 tablespoons hemp seeds

2 tablespoons all-natural peanut butter

2 cups kale, leaves only, tightly packed

1 pitted Medjool date

1   Wash and prep all ingredients.

2   Blend and serve.

# inflammation heavyweight

Tame inflammation's flames—and do your taste buds a favor—by indulging in this scrumptious blend. It harnesses the anti-inflammatory properties of not one, but five different foods.

Makes 2 Servings (16 to 20 Ounces)

¾ cup blueberries, frozen

½ cup cherries, frozen

1½ cups almond milk (page 274) or nondairy milk of choice

2 tablespoons shelled hemp seeds

¼ teaspoon cinnamon

1 cup spinach, tightly packed

1   Wash and prep all ingredients.

2   Blend and serve.

# energy shake

As my grandma would say, this recipe "charges my batteries." What's more energizing than a sweet blend of hydrating watermelon and banana? The latter provides magnesium and potassium—electrolytes that can help you to stay hydrated (and being well hydrated means avoiding gnarly headaches, fatigue, dry skin, and other symptoms that zap your zest). Pumpkin seeds provide protein and iron—both helpful energy enhancers—as well as satiating healthy fats.

### Makes 2 Servings (16 to 20 Ounces)

1 banana, frozen

1 cup watermelon chunks

1½ cups cashew hemp milk (page 276) or nondairy milk of choice

2 tablespoons pumpkin seeds

1 cup kale, leaves only, tightly packed

1   Wash and prep all ingredients.

2   Blend and serve.

THE BODY BOOSTERS

# sweet sustenance

If you like oatmeal cookies as much as I do, you'll love this recipe. Rolled oats add a thick creamy texture and are also rich in soluble fiber, which can help you feel full for a super long time. The recipe gets a flavor boost from ground cinnamon and a touch of sweetness from lucuma powder.

**PRO TIP** Lucuma is a fruit native to Peru, and powder derived from the fruit has a mildly sweet flavor that hovers somewhere between butterscotch and vanilla. As an added bonus, it can be used as a low-glycemic sweetener. You can find the powder at health-food stores and online; I like Navitas Naturals and Sunfoods brands.

### Makes 2 Servings (20 to 24 Ounces)

**1 banana, frozen**

**⅓ cup rolled oats**

**2 tablespoons almond butter**

**¼ teaspoon cinnamon**

**1 tablespoon lucuma powder**

**1½ cups cashew hemp milk (page 276) or nondairy milk of choice**

1   Wash and prep all ingredients.

2   Blend and serve.

# berry protein power

Berries and chocolate are like Fred and Ginger—a beloved pair. Hemp seeds and kale make this smoothie especially nutrient dense, plus the combination of banana and almond milk make it oh-so-creamy.

Makes 2 Servings (20 to 24 Ounces)

**1 large banana, frozen**

**1 cup blueberries, frozen**

**1½ cups almond milk (page 274) or nondairy milk of choice**

**2 tablespoons hemp seeds**

**2 tablespoons cacao nibs**

**1 cup kale, leaves only, tightly packed**

1   Wash and prep all ingredients.

2   Blend and serve.

# pumpkin power

Hello Thanksgiving! This festive fall smoothie calls for an irresistible mixture of pumpkin puree, frozen banana, pumpkin pie spice, and homemade almond milk. (Store bought is fine in this recipe, too, though the homemade version will be creamier!)

**PRO TIP** Don't have pumpkin pie spice? Make your own by combining ¼ teaspoon ground cinnamon, ⅛ teaspoon ground nutmeg, and ⅛ teaspoon ground allspice.

Makes 2 Servings (16 to 20 Ounces)

**1 cup pumpkin puree (see sidebar)**

**1 banana, frozen**

**1½ cups almond milk (page 274) or nondairy milk of choice**

**½ teaspoon pumpkin pie spice**

**½ teaspoon vanilla extract or the seeds of 1 vanilla bean, scraped**

**1 tablespoon almond butter**

**1 pitted Medjool date**

1   Wash and prep all ingredients.

2   Blend and serve.

## PUMPKIN PUREE

You can make your own pumpkin puree by cutting the stem off of a medium or large sugar pumpkin, scooping out the seeds, and cutting the pumpkin into quarters or sixths. Roast the pieces in an oven set to 350 degrees Fahrenheit for 45 minutes or so, or until you can pierce them very easily with a fork. Scoop the flesh out of the pumpkin skin, and place it into a food processor or a high-speed blender. Process the mixture till it's smooth.

If this sounds like too much legwork, don't worry: you can purchase organic pumpkin puree in most grocery stores. Just be sure not to accidentally pick up pumpkin pie filling, which is presweetened. My favorite is the Farmer's Market Foods brand, which also sells sweet potato puree and butternut squash puree—both of which will also work well in this smoothie!

# salted almond shake

Something about this salty sweet shake makes me think about beachside boardwalks and the fragrant roasted nut stands at Coney Island. It's a perfect example of how only a few plant-based ingredients can come together to create something that's every bit as satisfying as your favorite milkshake, but considerably healthier.

Almonds are an excellent source of vitamin E, which is associated with healthy, dewy skin, and they're also packed with protein. Feel free to adjust the Medjool dates in this recipe to suit your sweet tooth; you may find that one (or none) is enough for you!

Makes 2 Servings (16 to 20 Ounces)

**1 large banana, frozen**

**2 tablespoons almond butter**

**1½ cups almond milk (page 274) or nondairy milk of choice**

**⅛ teaspoon sea salt**

**1 to 2 pitted Medjool dates**

1  Wash and prep all ingredients.

2  Blend and serve.

THE BODY BOOSTERS

# mint chip champion

If you like classic Girl Scout cookies, you'll love this smoothie. It's a minty, chocolatey bonanza! It's also packed with anti-inflammatory spinach, antioxidant rich cacao nibs, and my creamy, protein-packed cashew hemp milk. It even has a spunky, mint green color and loads of leafy green goodness.

**PRO TIP** If you don't have cacao nibs at home, don't sweat it. They add some delightful texture to the smoothie, but one tablespoon of regular ole cocoa powder (or raw cacao powder, if that's what you've got) is a fine substitute.

Makes 2 Servings (20 to 24 Ounces)

1½ cups spinach, tightly packed

2 bananas, frozen

1 to 2 pitted Medjool dates

2 tablespoons mint leaves

1½ tablespoons cacao nibs

2 cups cashew hemp milk (page 276), or nondairy milk of choice

1   Wash and prep all ingredients.

2   Blend till smooth and serve.

THE BODY BOOSTERS

# for the love of nog

This smoothie, which first appeared in *Crazy Sexy Kitchen*, will make you the most popular guest at any holiday party. It's sweet, a little spicy, and every bit as creamy and delicious as traditional nog (without the dairy, refined sugar, and booze). Nutmeg is a tummy soother, which means that you can indulge in this decadent treat while also keeping your digestive system happy.

Makes 2 Servings (24 to 30 Ounces)

**3 cups almond milk (page 274) or nondairy milk of choice**

**1 banana**

**½ teaspoon freshly grated nutmeg (using Microplane or other grater)**

**½ tablespoon cinnamon**

**1 teaspoon almond extract**

**2 pitted Medjool dates**

1   Wash and prep all ingredients.

2   Blend till smooth and serve.

# THE AGE DEFIERS

The smoothies in this section allow the naturally potent antioxidant content of fresh fruits and vegetables to shine through. These fruity-tasting blends are rich in colorful phytonutrients, which will help to keep your skin glowing, your energy levels strong, and your spirits spry. Think facelift in a glass.

# watermelon quencher

Don't let the simplicity of this blend fool you. The combination of mint, watermelon, and banana is divine, and the drink is a powerful boost for your skin and energy. Watermelon is about 92 percent water, which—combined with the electrolytes from coconut water in this recipe—will help to keep you hydrated no matter how hot the day. As a beautifying added bonus, watermelon is also a great source of lycopene, which helps to protect against free radical damage and aging.

Makes 2 Servings (20 to 24 Ounces)

**1 banana, frozen**
**½ cucumber**
**1 cup watermelon cubes**
**1¼ cups coconut water**
**1 tablespoon mint leaves**

1  Wash and prep all ingredients.
2  Blend and serve.

THE AGE DEFIERS

# strawberry fields

This refreshing blend is one of my favorites from *Crazy Sexy Kitchen*. I love the way that lemon zest and orange brighten the smoothie (and infuse it with immunity boosting vitamin C). Strawberries also contribute vitamin C (a whopping 150 percent of your recommended daily allowance per serving) along with folic acid, which can help to regulate blood pressure and prevent anemia. Finally, these gorgeous berries provide the phytonutrient ellagic acid, which is thought to help keep the collagen in your skin healthy. Cheers!

Makes 2 Servings (24 to 30 Ounces)

3 cups cashew hemp milk (page 276) or nondairy milk of choice
2 cups fresh strawberries
1 tablespoon lemon zest
1 small orange, peeled
1 small banana
1½ cups loosely packed spinach

1   Wash and prep all ingredients.
2   Blend till smooth and serve.

# berry beautiful

We don't always associate fresh herbs (like basil, cilantro, or tarragon) with smoothies, but they can add tremendous flavor and freshness. Case in point: this beautiful, deep purple blend, which features a mixture of blueberries, blackberries, and basil. This is summer in a blender, and it's best when you use berries and basil that are at the peak of freshness.

**PRO TIP** Blackberry seeds can defy even the most powerful blenders (and teeth!), so no worries if they don't disappear into your smoothie. Enjoy the texture, and remember that plant fiber will do wonders for your digestion.

### Makes 2 Servings (20 to 24 Ounces)

1 small banana, frozen

½ cup blueberries, frozen

⅓ cup blackberries, frozen

¼ small Hass avocado

1½ cups Brazil nut milk (page 287) or nondairy milk of choice

1 teaspoon flax seeds, ground

1 cup kale, leaves only, tightly packed

1 tablespoon basil leaves (optional)

1   Wash and prep all ingredients.

2   Blend and serve.

# green honey

This creamy fresh blend is light and lovely. It makes me so happy. So I say, smoothie, get in my tummy! Stat!

A word about using coconut milk in smoothies: a little goes a long way. Though coconut milk is incredibly rich in medium chain fatty acids that have awesome antibacterial and antiviral properties, it's also rich in fat, so use it in moderation (¼ cup of full fat, canned coconut milk is a good amount). You can blend it with coconut water for a lighter consistency.

**PRO TIP** Coconut milk is typically sold in two forms: in a can or from a carton (which is lighter and less fatty). I prefer the canned stuff, because it's most authentic. You can use a lower-fat version of canned coconut milk, depending on what you prefer.

Makes 2 Servings (20 to 24 Ounces)

**3 cups honeydew melon cubes**

**4 ounces canned coconut milk (full or reduced fat)**

**1 cup coconut water**

**1½ cups spinach, tightly packed**

**2 tablespoons mint leaves**

1 Wash and prep all ingredients.

2 Blend till smooth and serve.

# chocolate avocado

One of my favorite raw food desserts is chocolate avocado pudding (don't be grossed out; it's actually a surprisingly delicious treat). I like to think of this smoothie as the sip-worthy version of that fabulous recipe. This is a perfect goodie when chocolate cravings pay a visit!

### Makes 2 Servings (20 to 24 Ounces)

**2 small bananas, frozen**

**1 to 2 pitted Medjool dates**

**1½ tablespoons cacao powder**

**¼ Hass avocado**

**1¾ cup almond milk (page 274) or nondairy milk of choice**

**½ teaspoon vanilla extract**

**1 cup baby spinach, tightly packed**

1   Wash and prep all ingredients.

2   Blend till smooth and serve.

# creamsicle

This smoothie pays homage to my favorite Popsicle—without the corn syrup and artificial flavors. You'll be amazed at how well it captures the sweet, refreshing taste we all remember, and unlike the original childhood treat, it's brimming with vitamin C, potassium, and healthy fats. What's not to love?

Makes 2 Servings (16 to 20 Ounces)

1 orange, peeled, pith removed, and cut into quarters

1 banana, frozen

½ teaspoon vanilla extract or powder

⅛ cup raw cashews

1½ cups cashew hemp milk (page 276) or nondairy milk of choice

1   Wash and prep all ingredients.

2   Blend till smooth and serve.

# tropical tonic

Kick off your flip-flops, grab a beach chair, and whip up this breezy beverage. This enlivening blend of tropical fruits is also a powerful beauty booster. Kiwi contains more vitamin C than any other fruit. Vitamin C helps to protect against free radical damage (which means fewer wrinkles for you), and it also aids in collagen formation, which means a firm, toned complexion.

**PRO TIP** Kiwi seeds house some essential fatty acids, so feel free to blend it up whole. If you want to make this smoothie a little creamier, try substituting your favorite nut milk in place of the water.

### Makes 2 Servings (20 to 24 Ounces)

**1 banana, frozen**

**1 kiwi, peeled**

**1 cup pineapple cubes**

**½ cucumber**

**1½ cups kale, leaves only, tightly packed**

**1½ cups water**

1   Wash and prep all ingredients.

2   In a high-speed blender, blend all ingredients. Serve.

# arugula antistresser

We all know and love arugula as a salad base, but there's more to this leafy green than meets the eye. Arugula can help to lower inflammation, protect our cells from UVA damage, and it's rich in vitamin K, which is important for bone health. Arugula is also loaded with folate, which can stimulate production of dopamine, a mood-boosting neurotransmitter. Hello, happy! Use this spicy sweet smoothie as a delicious way to lift your spirits, fight off inflammation-causing cortisol, and de-stress.

Makes 2 Servings (20 to 24 Ounces)

**1 cup arugula, tightly packed**
**½ small cucumber, peeled**
**2 pears, cored and seeded**
**¼ Hass avocado**
**1½ cups coconut water**

1  Wash and prep all ingredients.
2  Blend till smooth and serve.

# deep blue beauty

Hey, gorgeous, I bet I'm not the first person to tell you about acai, a super berry that hails from South and Central America. Acai is full of powerful antioxidants, as well as complete proteins. Unfortunately, a lot of the commercial juices and bottled beverages that feature acai are packed with artificial ingredients or sweeteners.

**PRO TIP** You can purchase unsweetened acai smoothie packs from the Sambazon brand (just check labels for the unsweetened flavor). Acai has a rich, unusual, and only mildly sweet flavor, so it's helpful to whirl it up with sweet bananas and berries. I like to use my creamy Brazil nut milk (page 287) in this smoothie, but commercial nondairy milk is a fine substitute if you don't have any on hand.

Makes 2 Servings (16 to 20 Ounces)

1 banana, frozen

½ pack (50 grams, or 1¾ ounces) unsweetened frozen acai pulp

½ cup blueberries, frozen

1½ cups spinach, packed

1 tablespoon coconut oil or coconut butter

2 teaspoons raw cacao powder

1 pitted Medjool date

1½ cups Brazil nut milk (page 287)

1 teaspoon spirulina or blue-green algae

1   Wash and prep all ingredients.

2   Blend and serve.

THE AGE DEFIERS

# raspberry revitalizer

This delicious smoothie will make you feel as though you're drinking dessert through a straw—but it'll also help to boost your vitality with healthful fatty acids and greens.

**PRO TIP** Coconut butter adds a wonderful creaminess and subtly decadent flavor to smoothies—a nice departure from almond or peanut butter, if those are your go-to's. It can be a little tricky to find, but you should be able to get your hands on some at most health-food stores or online.

### Makes 2 Servings (20 to 24 Ounces)

**1 cup kale, tightly packed**

**1 cup raspberries, frozen**

**1 banana, frozen**

**1 tablespoon coconut butter or coconut oil**

**½ teaspoon vanilla extract**

**1¾ cups Brazil nut milk (page 287) or nondairy milk of choice**

1   Wash and prep all ingredients.

2   Blend till smooth and serve.

# hangover helper

Did ya party a little too hardy? Kiss that headache good-bye with this little helper. This delicious blend features tons of hydrating foods to help get you back on your feet—including potassium-rich banana, cucumber, and coconut water. It also features some healthy fats in the form of creamy avocado to lift your energy levels, and plenty of leafy greens and lemons to help your body cleanse and detox.

Makes 2 Servings (16 to 20 Ounces)

½ banana, frozen

1 cup honeydew melon, cubed

½ cucumber, peeled

½ cup watercress, leaves and top parts of stems, tightly packed

1 cup spinach, tightly packed

2 tablespoons parsley, tightly packed

½-inch piece ginger, peeled

2 teaspoons lemon juice

¼ Hass avocado

1½ cups coconut water

1   Wash and prep all ingredients.

2   Blend till smooth and serve.

# cherry chocolate bliss

Love chocolate-covered cherries? Then this smoothie is for you. I'm cuckoo for the combination of raw cacao, creamy avocado, almond milk, and sweet cherries—it's like dessert in a glass, in the best of ways. I also love that the smoothie is bursting with anthocyanins, plant pigments that give cherries their beautiful color and help keep our skin strong (while also warding off inflammation).

And because the best desserts are as healthy as they are delicious, I've thrown in some nutrient-rich leafy greens in the form of spinach (though you're welcome to use your favorite green here instead!).

### Makes 2 Servings (16 to 20 Ounces)

**1½ cups spinach, tightly packed**
**1 cup cherries, frozen**
**1 banana, frozen**
**¼ Hass avocado**
**1 tablespoon raw cacao powder**
**1½ cups almond milk (page 274) or nondairy milk of choice**

1   Wash and prep all ingredients.
2   Blend and serve.

# THE SUPERHEROES

The following blends are unexpected and invigorating. They're also functional. Many of them are infused with superfoods, like maca, cacao, or matcha powder. These unique ingredients can help our bodies with repair, energy production, healing, hormone balance, and a host of other vital functions (for more on superfoods, see page 85).

These blends cover a vast array of texture, taste, and use: some, like my "Quick Recovery" smoothie, are light and fruity, while others, like my "All Day Energy" shake, are creamy and rich. My hope is that they'll inspire you to think outside the smoothie box!

# hot flash healer

Lady, no need to open a window in the dead of winter—maca to the rescue! In this smoothie, hormone-balancing maca tangos with the natural phytoestrogens in flax seed, which are thought to help relieve menopause symptoms.

Makes 2 Servings (16 to 20 Ounces)

1½ cups strawberries, frozen

1 apple, cored and seeded

1 tablespoon flax seeds, ground

1 teaspoon maca powder

1½ cups macadamia maple milk (page 277) or nondairy milk of choice

1   Wash and prep all ingredients.

2   Blend and serve.

# HORMO

*I don't know about*

'70s. Back in my groc
ing bras for their ne
thirteen or fourteen
"period party" cele
nese restaurant (ju
kids as young as
son–stacked rug
it's dangerous. L

Steroids are
beef, pork, an
make the ani
hormones? Y
year round,
mones so s
lactating—
such an u

She's
growth k
duction,
hormo
3, is li
tory,
inter

# hormone helper

Our Crazy Sexy hormones are in flux all throughout our lifecycles: for ladies, this includes puberty, childbirth, and menopause. While hormonal changes can often create bodily ouchies, nature graciously provides certain nutrients that can help to lessen the dreaded aches, pains, and hot flashes.

**PRO TIP** Phytoestrogens, a class of phytonutrients found in soy, flax, and sesame seeds, can gently mimic the effects of estrogen in the body, helping to lessen the symptoms of PMS and menopause. You'll find plenty of them, along with libido-enhancing maca, in this creamy smoothie. On page 77, you'll find instructions for how to open a young Thai coconut. You can also use a frozen brand, like Exotic Superfoods. If you don't have a source for young Thai coconut, try using ¼ avocado in this recipe instead.

Makes 2 Servings (20 to 24 Ounces)

1 banana, frozen

½ cup blueberries, frozen

½ cup young Thai coconut meat

1¾ cups Brazil nut milk (page 287) or nondairy milk of choice

1 teaspoon flax seeds, ground

1 teaspoon maca

1 cup spinach, tightly packed

1    Wash and prep all ingredients.

2    Blend and serve.

# digestive fire

All these ingredients add up to awesome. In the Ayurvedic tradition, the body's digestive power is imagined as fire, or Agni. Stoke your digestive furnace with this smoothie, which features belly-soothing mint, inflammation-taming ginger, electrolyte-balancing banana, and the natural digestive, pineapple. Pineapple is an excellent source of the enzyme bromelain, which digests protein. It may give your digestive system a powerful boost. Some studies have suggested that bromelain may help to ease symptoms of osteoarthritis as well.

Makes 2 Servings (16 to 20 Ounces)

**1 banana, frozen**

**1 cup pineapple chunks, frozen**

**1½ cups coconut water**

**1 cup kale, tightly packed**

**2 tablespoons fresh mint, chopped**

**¾-inch piece of ginger, peeled**

1 Wash and prep all ingredients.

2 Blend and serve.

# morning jolt

Okay, so this smoothie can be a wee bit more demanding, because it involves making fresh carrot juice and then blending it into a (blissful) smoothie. If the idea of using two appliances sends you running, then just keep this smoothie on the back burner for a leisurely weekend morning. Once you try it, I promise you won't mind the extra elbow grease; the combination of carrot, banana, and ginger is ah-mazing. Plus, a boost of maca and cashews means that this smoothie can sustain your energy all the way to lunchtime.

### Makes 2 Servings (16 to 20 Ounces)

1 cup carrot juice

½ cup coconut water

1 large banana, frozen

½-inch piece of ginger, peeled

¼ cup cashews

1 teaspoon maca powder

1   Wash and prep all ingredients.

2   Blend and serve.

# all day energy

This smoothie is creamy, filling, and designed to help keep your energy levels stable and strong throughout the day. Matcha is a form of stone-ground green tea leaves. It's thought to have all of the antioxidant benefits of green tea, but in a more concentrated form. In addition to its energy enhancing qualities, matcha is associated with mood regulation, increased metabolism, and antioxidant power. It makes a wonderful addition to smoothies (especially if you're trying to kick the coffee habit).

**PRO TIP** In this blend, matcha plays deliciously well with avocado, banana, and vanilla. I recommend using homemade almond milk or cashew hemp milk in this smoothie if you can; they really enhance the taste!

Makes 2 Servings (16 to 20 Ounces)

**1 teaspoon matcha green tea powder**

**¼ ripe avocado**

**1 banana, frozen**

**1½ cups almond milk (page 274) or cashew hemp milk (page 276)**

**2 teaspoons maple syrup or 1 pitted Medjool date**

**½ teaspoon vanilla extract**

1   Wash and prep all ingredients.

2   Blend till smooth and serve.

THE SUPERHEROES

# antioxidant boost

This smoothie is an antioxidant, free-radical busting, inflammation-fighting superhero! You could literally serve it in a cape and tights. Goji berries, which have been used for years in Traditional Chinese Medicine, are a complete source of protein and provide iron, zinc, and vitamin C along with their incredible phytonutrient stores. The catechin EGCG, which is abundant in matcha powder, is associated with a reduced risk of cancer (and the little boost of caffeine will perk you up, too). See, I told ya it was a superhero in disguise. To your health!

Makes 2 Servings (16 to 20 Ounces)

**1 cup mixed berries, frozen**

**½ cup blueberries, frozen**

**¼ cup goji berries**

**1½ cups cashew hemp milk (page 276) or nondairy milk of choice**

**½ teaspoon matcha green tea powder**

**1 cup spinach, tightly packed**

1 Wash and prep all ingredients.

2 Blend and serve.

# move it!

This blend is packed with ingredients that can soothe achy joints and body pains. Cherries have powerful anti-inflammatory properties, and the phytonutrients in their deep red skins, called anthocyanins, are associated with antiaging properties. Cinnamon, turmeric, and flax are also inflammation fighters, and they give the smoothie a wonderfully complex flavor.

**PRO TIP** If you don't have time to whip up turmeric milk, don't sweat it. You can use your favorite store-bought nondairy milk and add a half-teaspoon of dried turmeric powder to the mix instead!

Makes 2 Servings (16 to 20 Ounces)

½ banana, frozen

½ cup cherries, frozen

¾ cup blueberries, frozen

1 tablespoon almond butter

1 tablespoon flax seeds, ground

¼ teaspoon cinnamon

1 cup spinach or kale, tightly packed

1½ cups turmeric milk (page 283) or nondairy milk of choice

1   Wash and prep all ingredients.

2   Blend and serve.

# aztec spirit

This recipe is a *Crazy Sexy Kitchen* classic. It's a fiery and chocolatey blend that will help you get your kale on in a sneakily delicious form. Be mindful of your cayenne pinch, because a little goes a long way. If you don't happen to have espresso, just brew a cup of superstrong coffee and use it instead. Coffee isn't a daily addition to smoothies at Casa Carr, but it can add a wonderful jolt of flavor and energy once in a while.

### Makes 2 Servings (24 to 30 Ounces)

3 cups Brazil nut milk (page 287) or nondairy milk of choice

⅓ cup cacao powder

¾ teaspoon vanilla extract or the seeds of 1 vanilla bean, scraped

2 shots of espresso or very strong coffee (optional)

2 tablespoons maple syrup

3 kale leaves, stripped from the stem

Pinch of cayenne pepper

1   Wash and prep all ingredients.

2   Blend till smooth and serve.

# brain booster

Blueberries aren't just a delicious way to sweeten your smoothies (and give them a gorgeous, deep blue hue). They're also powerful brain boosters. In clinical studies, blueberries have been associated with increased cognitive function, including memory improvement, and they may also help to protect your brain from oxidative stress, lessening the risk of Alzheimer's disease and dementia. The omega-3 fatty acids in walnuts are also associated with cognitive protection, and a possible mood lift: omega-3's are thought to help fight depression. Who knew there could be so much power in your glass? (You did!).

Makes 2 Servings (16 to 20 Ounces)

½ banana, frozen

1½ cups blueberries, frozen

1½ cups almond milk (page 274) or nondairy milk of choice

2 tablespoons walnuts, chopped

1 cup kale, leaves only, tightly packed

½ teaspoon cinnamon, ground

1   Wash and prep all ingredients.

2   Blend and serve.

# ginger chia supercharger

Supercharger is right. This smoothie packs in protein from chia seeds, almond milk, almond butter, and kale, which makes it a perfect go-to before or after a workout. I love the combination of ginger, mango, and almond—it tastes decadent but fruity and uplifting at the same time.

**PRO TIP** If you don't have mango, substitute pineapple or extra banana instead. Or, for a very different—but also very delicious—blend, try swapping blueberries for mango.

Makes 2 Servings (20 to 24 Ounces)

**1 cup kale, leaves only, tightly packed**

**1 banana, frozen**

**1 cup mango, frozen and cubed**

**½-inch piece ginger, peeled**

**1 teaspoon chia seeds**

**1 tablespoon almond butter**

**1¾ cups almond milk (page 274) or nondairy milk of choice**

1    Wash and prep all ingredients.

2    Blend till smooth and serve.

# mood lift

When I need to lift my spirits, this smoothie is my go-to pick-me-up. Chocolate probably boosts your mood by virtue of its rich and swanky flavor. But that's not the only reason we associate it with all sorts of blissful feelings. Cocoa (or its raw form, cacao) signals the brain to release neurotransmitters that stimulate feelings of euphoria. It also contains a higher concentration of antioxidants than any other food we know of, which means that it's an age-defying powerhouse. Can you believe it? Certain types of chocolate are actually good for you (how's that for lifting your mood?).

Makes 2 Servings (16 to 20 Ounces)

**1 banana, frozen**
**1½ tablespoons cacao powder**
**1 teaspoon cinnamon**
**1 tablespoon lucuma powder**
**1 pitted Medjool date**
**1¾ cups almond milk (page 274) or nondairy milk of choice**

1   Wash and prep all ingredients.

2   Blend and serve.

# quick recovery

This blend is designed to help your body rebound and recover from stress—including the wear and tear of exercise. It's full of anti-inflammatory ingredients, including coconut oil, ginger, and turmeric. It's also hydrating, thanks to coconut water and potassium-packed banana. Drink up after an extended run, a grueling flight, or a tough work week.

### Makes 2 Servings (16 to 20 Ounces)

**1 banana, frozen**

**1 cup mango chunks, frozen**

**½-inch piece turmeric, peeled**

**¾-inch piece ginger, peeled**

**1 cup spinach, tightly packed**

**1 tablespoon coconut oil or coconut butter**

**1½ cups coconut water**

1    Wash and prep all ingredients.

2    Blend and serve.

THE SUPERHEROES

# 9

# RADIANT NUT AND SEED MILKS

# basic nut milk formula

I've listed quite a few nut milk recipes in this chapter, but I also wanted to give you a basic recipe that will work with many different nuts. Here's a basic formula to get you started.

**PRO TIP** I like to use Medjool dates, which contain minerals and anti-oxidants along with natural sugar, but maple syrup, coconut syrup, and yacon syrup also work well as sweeteners.

Yields 4 Cups

**1 cup nuts, soaked overnight and rinsed**

**3 to 4 cups filtered water (depending on how creamy a blend you'd like)**

**A pinch of salt**

**Sweetener to taste**

1   Blend the mixture thoroughly, until it looks totally uniform and frothy (a few minutes). To strain, you can use a double layer of cheesecloth or a nut milk bag. Nut milk bags are a great and inexpensive investment (they retail for about $8 to $10 on Amazon, at Bed Bath & Beyond, or at your local health food store), and they make it even easier to create perfectly smooth nut milks at home. Hold your nut milk bag or your cheesecloth over a large bowl, and pour the unstrained nut milk through. Use the bag or cloth to squeeze the contents thoroughly, making sure to extract every drop! Store your nut milk in an airtight container in the fridge for up to 3 or 4 days.

RADIANT NUT AND SEED MILKS

# almond milk

There are oodles of recipes for homemade almond milk, but this is my tried-and-true classic. Medjool dates add a hint of sweetness, and vanilla makes it perfect for smoothies. If you want less sweet almond milk for soups or other savory recipes, omit the dates and vanilla, or adjust them to taste. Straining the almond milk with a nut milk bag or cheesecloth makes it silky smooth.

Yields 4 Cups

**1 cup almonds, soaked 8 hours**

**2 to 3 pitted Medjool dates**

**¼ teaspoon salt**

**1 teaspoon vanilla extract or the seeds of 1 vanilla bean, scraped**

**4 cups water**

1   In a high-speed blender, blend all ingredients till totally smooth.

2   Create a large, double layer of cheesecloth and hold it over a large mixing bowl, or hold a nut milk bag over a large mixing bowl. Pour the almond milk through the cheesecloth or bag and squeeze thoroughly. You can compost or discard the nut pulp. Transfer the nut milk to an airtight container. It will keep in the fridge for about 3 days.

## SOAKING NUTS AND SEEDS

Nuts and seeds will blend up more easily if you soak them in water first. The necessary soak times vary according to the nut or seed you're using; larger and harder nuts tend to require more time. Here are some approximate soak times for the nuts and seeds you'll see in my nut milk recipes.

ALMONDS: 8 hours (or overnight)

BRAZIL NUTS: 4 hours

CASHEWS: 2 hours (or up to 4)

MACADAMIA NUTS: 2 hours (or up to 4)

PUMPKIN SEEDS: 8 hours (or overnight)

SESAME SEEDS: 8 hours (or overnight)

WALNUTS: 4 hours

To soak, simply place the raw nuts or seeds in a large mixing bowl and add enough water to cover them 2 to 3 inches. After soaking, rinse the nuts/seeds in a colander or sieve and allow them to drain completely before blending. Voilà!

# cashew hemp milk

This is my go-to nut milk blend. It's delicious, easy to prepare, and it's got an awesome boost of protein, thanks to the addition of hemp seeds. This coupled with healthy fats from the cashews makes the milk an ideal addition to juice cleanses or liquid reboots.

**PRO TIP** Hemp seeds can have a slightly bitter taste, so I typically use more dates in this recipe. Feel free to adjust the quantity of dates according to your taste buds and health needs.

Yields 4½ Cups

⅔ cup cashews, soaked for 2 hours

¼ cup shelled hemp seeds

2 to 3 pitted Medjool dates

¼ teaspoon salt

1 teaspoon vanilla extract or the seeds of 1 vanilla bean, scraped

4 cups water

1   In a high-speed blender, blend all ingredients till totally smooth. Store in an airtight container in the fridge for up to four days.

# macadamia maple milk

I'll have a tall glass of pleasure and so will you with this recipe. Talk about decadent. Macadamia nuts can be expensive, so I make this heavenly nut milk as a special treat, and I savor every sip (without sharing!).

Yields 4½ Cups

**1 cup raw macadamia nuts, soaked for 2 hours**

**3¾ cups water**

**¼ teaspoon salt**

**1 teaspoon pure maple extract
(I like the Frontier Natural Products brand)**

**2 tablespoons maple syrup**

**1 teaspoon vanilla extract**

1   In a high-speed blender, blend nuts and water for 2 to 3 minutes, or until the mixture is completely smooth.

2   Create a large, double layer of cheesecloth and hold it over a large mixing bowl, or hold a nut milk bag over a large mixing bowl. Pour the macadamia milk through the cheesecloth or bag and squeeze thoroughly. You can compost or discard the nut pulp. Transfer the nut milk to an airtight container.

3   Once you've strained the nut milk, return the milk to your blender and blend in the salt, maple extracts, maple syrup, and vanilla. Store the macadamia milk in an airtight container in the fridge for about 3 days.

# chocolate almond milk

Your inner kiddo will go nuts for this milk. Grab some graham crackers and cuddle up with your books as you sip on this wonderful, dairy-free treat.

**PRO TIP** You don't have to use cacao powder in this recipe—cocoa powder will work, too—but cacao powder tends to be more potent than cocoa powder, and I love the way its bold flavor comes to life in this recipe. I also like to add a little bit of cinnamon, but feel free to leave it out if you prefer your almond milk on the super traditional side.

### Yields 3½ to 4 Cups

**1 cup almonds, soaked for 8 hours**

**2 to 3 pitted Medjool dates**

**¼ teaspoon salt**

**4 cups water**

**2 tablespoons cacao powder**

**¼ teaspoon cinnamon (optional)**

1   In a high-speed blender, blend the almonds, dates, salt, and water till totally smooth.

2   Create a large, double layer of cheesecloth and hold it over a large mixing bowl, or hold a nut milk bag over a large mixing bowl. Pour the almond milk through the cheesecloth or bag and squeeze thoroughly. You can compost or discard the nut pulp.

3   Transfer strained almond milk back to your blender. Add the cacao and cinnamon, if using. Blend till smooth.

4   Transfer the nut milk to an airtight container. It will keep in the fridge for about 3 days.

# cashew chai milk

"Get your chai on!" as Oprah would say. This recipe is sweet, spicy, and all-around divine. It's wonderful blended up with fresh banana and greens, and it also pairs well with tropical fruits. For a creamy evening treat, warm a cup over the stovetop, sprinkle with cinnamon, and sip to your heart's content.

### Yields 3¾ Cups

**1 cup raw cashews, soaked for 2 hours, rinsed, and drained**

**½-inch piece ginger, peeled**

**1 teaspoon cinnamon**

**¼ teaspoon cardamom**

**¼ teaspoon salt**

**2 to 3 tablespoons maple syrup**

**3¼ cups water**

1   In a high-speed blender, blend all ingredients till creamy and smooth. Store in an airtight container for up to three days in the fridge.

2 Cup

1 3/4

1 1/2

1    1 1/4
     Cup

3/4

1/2

1/4

# turmeric milk

Turmeric in your milk? Are you cray cray? Yes! Don't tell the other nut milks, but this recipe is my favorite. Once upon a time, the only thing I knew about turmeric was that it had a brilliant yellow-orange color, which makes it a perfect addition to tofu scrambles. But with the right combination of supporting spices and sweetness, this turmeric twist is out of sight. Plus, it contains incredible anti-inflammatory properties. Turmeric milk can be served cold or warmed on the stovetop for an after-dinner treat.

Yields 3½ Cups

3 cups almond milk (page 274)

4 ounces canned coconut milk (full or reduced fat)

1½ teaspoons turmeric powder or 1-inch fresh turmeric root, peeled

½-inch piece ginger, peeled

½ teaspoon cinnamon

¼ teaspoon cardamom

2 tablespoons maple syrup

1   Blend all ingredients together in a blender till smooth. Store in an airtight container in the fridge for up to 4 days.

RADIANT NUT AND SEED MILKS

# green milk

I know what you're thinking: green milk?! It may seem like a nutty idea, but why not infuse your go-to almond milk with a little green goodness? This milk is perfect for sipping, and if you use it in green smoothies, you'll be doubling up on plant power.

**PRO TIP** To make the milk, follow my basic almond milk formula, adding kale and spinach in the blending step. Then you strain and serve as you normally would. The resulting mixture is sweet and creamy, and even though you'll barely taste the veggies, your body will thank you for them!

Yields 4 Cups

**2 leaves kale, stems removed**

**2 cups baby spinach, packed**

**1 cup almonds, soaked for 8 hours**

**2 to 3 pitted Medjool dates**

**¼ teaspoon salt**

**1 teaspoon vanilla extract**

**4 cups water**

1   In a high-speed blender, blend all ingredients till totally smooth.

2   Create a large, double layer of cheesecloth and hold it over a large mixing bowl, or hold a nut milk bag over a large mixing bowl. Pour the green milk through the cheesecloth or bag and squeeze thoroughly. You can compost or discard the nut pulp. Transfer the nut milk to an airtight container. It will keep in the fridge for about 3 days.

# brazil nut milk

Talk about luxurious. If you could drink cashmere, this is how it would taste. Brazil nuts are an excellent source of selenium, a mineral with strong antioxidant properties. Groovy, no? More important, they make a super creamy and delicious nut milk. I use this one whenever I want a particularly rich flavor and texture.

### Yields 3½ to 4 Cups

**1 cup Brazil nuts, soaked for 4 hours**

**2 to 3 pitted Medjool dates**

**¼ teaspoon salt**

**1½ teaspoon vanilla extract or the seeds of 1 vanilla bean, scraped**

**4 cups water**

1   In a high-speed blender, blend all ingredients till totally smooth.

2   Create a large, double layer of cheesecloth and hold it over a large mixing bowl, or hold a nut milk bag over a large mixing bowl. Pour the Brazil nut milk through the cheesecloth or bag and squeeze thoroughly. You can compost or discard the nut pulp. Transfer the nut milk to an airtight container. It will keep in the fridge for about 3 days.

RADIANT NUT AND SEED MILKS

# pumpkin seed milk

Get this, seed milks have all of the yummy richness of regular nut milks, but they're ideal for those folks with tree nut allergies. They're also nutrient dense, like the pumpkin seeds in this recipe, which are brimming with zinc, protein, and iron. A touch of coconut oil adds flavor and silky smooth texture.

Yields 3 Cups

1 cup pumpkin seeds, soaked for 8 hours

2 to 3 pitted Medjool dates

¼ teaspoon salt

1 teaspoon vanilla extract

1 tablespoon coconut oil, melted

3½ cups water

1   In a high-speed blender, blend all ingredients till totally smooth.

2   Create a large, double layer of cheesecloth and hold it over a large mixing bowl, or hold a nut milk bag over a large mixing bowl. Pour the pumpkin seed milk through the cheesecloth or bag and squeeze thoroughly. Transfer the seed milk to an airtight container. It will keep in the fridge for about 3 days.

# sesame seed milk

Did you know that sesame seeds are a stellar source of calcium? One-quarter cup provides 35 percent of your daily recommended allowance—not too shabby. These tiny nutritional powerhouses are also rich in iron and protein, which makes them a dazzling addition to nutrient-dense smoothies—and a fantastic base for this creamy seed milk.

**PRO TIP** To make the sesame seed milk, I use my usual ratio of water, seeds, sweet Medjool dates, salt, and vanilla. You'll love the rich flavor of this blend!

### Yields 3½ to 4 Cups

**1 cup hulled sesame seeds, soaked for 8 hours**

**1 tablespoon melted coconut oil**

**2 to 3 pitted Medjool dates, to taste**

**¼ teaspoon sea salt**

**1 teaspoon vanilla extract or powder**

**4 cups water**

1   In a high-speed blender, blend all ingredients till totally smooth.

2   Create a large, double layer of cheesecloth and hold it over a large mixing bowl, or hold a nut milk bag over a large mixing bowl. Pour the sesame seed milk through the cheesecloth or bag and squeeze thoroughly. Transfer the seed milk to an airtight container. It will keep in the fridge for about 3 days.

RADIANT NUT AND SEED MILKS

**PART THREE**

# your three-day cleanse

In the following pages, you'll find my blueprint for a mind-clearing, soul-lifting, body-enlivening three-day reset.

As I mentioned earlier, this plan is for everyone: folks who are just getting started with juices and smoothies, juicing and blending pros, and those of you who love the taste of these drinks but sometimes find it challenging to stick with the habit. In the three days I've mapped out for you, you'll have a chance to ignite your love of clean nutrition. More important, you'll give your body the opportunity to soak in some easy-to-digest juices, blends, and meals. By the end of these three days, you should feel rejuvenated, focused, and inspired.

The point of this refresh is to restore—not to starve. Cleansing can actually be quite joyful. Fasting, on the other hand, can make you want to eat a sofa cushion slathered in butter. So with that in mind, I've given you two morning juices; a lunchtime blend; an afternoon juice, blend, or snack option; a healthy dinner; and a warm evening nut milk to savor. But if you find that you're hungry in spite of these options, don't hesitate to modify the plan and have a snack at any point. I've included a list of my ten favorite healthy snack options, which can all be enjoyed in addition to the options in the three-day plan. Lastly, make sure to drink plenty of water throughout each day.

To get started, use the grocery list provided to prep for your three-day adventure.

Then it's as easy as following along with the juices, smoothies, and meals listed. All of the recipes in bold are provided following the meal plan (they're listed right after the snacks).

During your three-day cleanse, you'll be taking a break from stimulating substances like coffee and alcohol. Don't worry; they'll be there for you when you're done—though you'll probably want to create a new relationship to them. Feel free to include herbal tea or green tea, if desired. You'll also step away from gluten and animal products, both of which can be irritating and taxing on your system. When we abruptly change our diets (like when we're cleansing) it's common to face some digestive disruption. Review my recommendations for constipation or loose stools (page 111) and all my self-care tips (pages 101–104). Epsom salt bath? Yup, it's got your name all over it!

Take some time to meditate, move your magnificent body, and reflect. Clear your calendar if possible (or at least pull back). Make space for your precious self. Juices, smoothies, and healthy foods are only part of the restorative process; in order to get the most benefit from this experience, you'll need to take care of both your body and spirit. At the end of this experience, you may be surprised at all the new ideas and ah-ha's that come rushing in as a result of some clean food and a clear head.

Drink up, rest up, and enjoy!

## YOUR THREE-DAY CLEANSE

**UPON RISING:** Warm water with a squeeze of lemon and ginger. Remember also to drink plenty of water throughout the day.

**8 A.M.:** 8 to 10 ounces (1 serving) Classic Green Lemonade (page 127)

**10:30 A.M.:** 8 to 10 ounces (1 serving) Tummy Tamer (page 157)

**1 P.M.:** 8 to 10 ounces (1 serving) Easygoing Green Smoothie (page 199)

**4 P.M.:** 8 to 10 ounces (1 serving) Blueberry Lemon-Aid (page 163) and snack of choice (choose from list of snack options, page 313)

**7 P.M.:** Large salad with raw or gently steamed vegetables of choice, 2 tablespoons raw pumpkin seeds, ½ cup **Herbed Lentils** (page 300), and 3 tablespoons **Lemon Tahini Dressing** (page 308)

**9 P.M.:** 8 ounces Turmeric Milk (page 283), warmed

## YOUR THREE-DAY CLEANSE

**UPON RISING:** Warm water with a squeeze of lemon and ginger. Remember also to drink plenty of water throughout the day.

**8 A.M.:** 8 to 10 ounces (1 serving) Rise 'n' Shine (page 173)

**10:30 A.M.:** 8 to 10 ounces (1 serving) Green Me Up (page 130)

**1 P.M.:** 8 to 10 ounces (1 serving) Inflammation Heavyweight (page 220)

**4 P.M.:** 8 to 10 ounces (1 serving) Savory Green Smoothie (page 206)

**7 P.M.:** 1 cup **Lemon Quinoa** (page 299) with 1 to 2 cups raw or steamed vegetables of choice, 2 tablespoons hemp seeds, and **Cilantro Lime Vinaigrette** (page 309)

**9 P.M.:** 8 ounces Chocolate Almond Milk (page 279), warmed

**UPON RISING:** Warm water with a squeeze of lemon and ginger. Remember also to drink plenty of water throughout the day.

**8 A.M.:** 8 to 10 ounces (1 serving) Pucker Up (page 177)

**10:30 A.M.:** 8 to 10 ounces (1 serving) Garden-in-a-Glass (page 142)

**1 P.M.:** 8 to 10 ounces (1 serving) Body Builder (page 219)

**4 P.M.:** 8 to 10 ounces (1 serving) Fatigue Fighter (page 193) and snack of choice (choose from list of snack options, page 313)

**7 P.M.:** 2 cups **Zucchini Noodles** (page 303), served raw or lightly sautéed in a teaspoon of olive oil, with ¼ cup **Cashew Cheese** (page 304), ½ cup **Herbed Lentils** (page 300), fresh chopped basil, and ⅓ cup **Raw Marinara** Sauce (page 305). Serve with extra steamed veggies if desired.

**9 P.M.:** 8 ounces Cashew Chai Milk (page 281), warmed